The Learning Self

The Jossey-Bass Higher and
Adult Education Series

The Learning Self

Understanding the Potential for Transformation

Mark Tennant

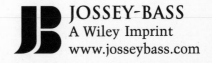

JOSSEY-BASS
A Wiley Imprint
www.josseybass.com

Published by Jossey-Bass
A Wiley Imprint
One Montgomery Street, Suite 1200, San Francisco, CA 94104-4594—www.josseybass.com

Jossey-Bass books and products are available through most bookstores. To contact Jossey-
Bass directly call our Customer Care Department within the U.S. at 800-956-7739, outside
the U.S. at 317-572-3986, or fax 317-572-4002.

Wiley publishes in a variety of print and electronic formats and by print-on-demand.
Some material included with standard print versions of this book may not be included
in e-books or in print-on-demand. If this book refers to media such as a CD or DVD that
is not included in the version you purchased, you may download this material at http://
booksupport.wiley.com. For more information about Wiley products, visit www.wiley.com.

S. Ashton excerpt in Chapter Two from "Authenticity in Adult Learning," *International
Journal of Lifelong Education*, 2010, 29(1), Taylor & Francis, Ltd., reprinted by permission
of the publisher (Taylor & Francis, Ltd., http://tandfonline.com).

Library of Congress Cataloging-in-Publication Data

Tennant, Mark.
    The learning self : understanding the potential for transformation /
Mark Tennant.—First edition.
        pages cm.—(The Jossey-Bass Higher and Adult Education Series)
    Includes bibliographical references and index.
        ISBN 978-0-470-39336-9 (hardback); ISBN 978-1-118-20674-4 (ebk.);
        ISBN 978-1-118-20675-(ebk.); ISBN 978-1-118-20676-8 (ebk.)
        1. Transformative learning. 2. Learning, Psychology of. 3. Adult learning.
I. Title.
LC1100.T46 2012
370.11'5—dc23

                                                        2011047499

Printed in the United States of America
FIRST EDITION
HB Printing 10 9 8 7 6 5 4 3 2 1

Contents

Preface

This book examines the kind of learning that brings about significant personal change. It is concerned with the various techniques, processes, and practices used to promote such learning, and their embedded assumptions about self and identity, how we are formed, and our capacity for change. As Foucault reminds us, "The main interest in life and work is to become someone else that you were not in the beginning" (quoted in Martin, 1988, p. 9). The techniques, processes, and practices, which entail a great deal of "self-work," have been referred to as "technologies of the self" (see Foucault, 1988b; Tennant, 1998). My interest in this subject is both academic and professional. My academic interest has been forged through my grounding in psychology, supplemented by my exposure to various critiques of psychology, especially the charge that it is a discipline and practice that functions to normalize people in a way that serves the interests of contemporary social and economic circumstances. My professional interest comes from a career in teaching in which I have formed the view that success as a teacher depends squarely on one's sense of self and professional identity. I agree with Palmer (1998) when he says, "My ability to connect with my students, and to connect them with the subject, depends less on the methods I use than on the degree to which I know and trust my selfhood—and am willing to make it available and vulnerable in the service of learning" (p. 10). No doubt this applies generally across the helping professions as well as to those who have management or leadership roles in their workplace. As a teacher, I have also come to realize that "any understanding of human learning must begin with the nature of the person" (Jarvis, 2005, p. 1; see also Jarvis, 2009). It is the whole self that is engaged in learning in the sense that learning encompasses the social, emotional, cognitive, and bodily dimensions of selfhood (see Jarvis, 2005; Illeris, 2002, 2005). But of course selfhood is a highly contested concept, and assumptions about selfhood cannot be entirely separated from the methods we use as teachers, advisers, counselors, or managers—indeed, such assumptions are arguably embedded in our everyday practices.

The purpose of this book is, first, to explore how different conceptualizations of selfhood serve to frame our understanding of personal change and, second, to elucidate the various processes or "technologies of the self" adopted by teachers and others in the helping professions to promote learning for personal change. I argue that the various interventions in the name of personal change contain within them explicit or implicit theoretical perspectives, which pose essentially different questions and cast the issues in different ways. However, there are two common issues that reoccur across all theoretical perspectives and practices. The first concerns whether we can participate in our own self-formation, the limits of this, and the extent to which our selves are socially and culturally constituted. The second concerns whether we can speak of coherent, continuous, and stable selves, or whether we should be properly speaking about fragmented, divided, and discontinuous selves.

The introductory chapter highlights the renewed focus on the self in contemporary life. It explores the key concepts of *self*, *identity*, and *subjectivity* and their meanings and functions in the academic literature. The remaining chapters fall into two distinct groups. The first group comprises chapters dealing with different versions of the self: The Authentic or Real Self, The Autonomous Self, The Repressed Self, The Socially Constructed Self, and The Storied Self. My aim in each case is to analyze the issues that each conception of the self presents and to briefly comment on the implications for learning for personal change. In the first part of The Authentic or Real Self I evaluate the arguments and empirical evidence suggesting that our biological inheritance is the source of our *real* self. In the second part I explore the conceptualization of the *authentic* self as being true to our general nature as human beings. In The Autonomous Self I trace the meanings given to autonomy and its preeminence in the psychological and educational literature as a goal that is a marker of both psychological health and individual empowerment. The Repressed Self presents key concepts in psychoanalysis, such as the unconscious, the divided nature of our mental life, and the sacrifices made by the self in order to participate in civilized life. I also provide a treatment of the implications of psychoanalysis and its applications to education. The Socially Constructed Self looks at theories of the self that argue that we are *world-open*—that is, our biological nature is such that we are open to being constructed by our social milieu (this includes changes to both our sense of self and our cognitive capacities). The final chapter in this group of chapters, The Storied Self, deals with a range of theories that use narrative as their explanatory tool, from the psychologically oriented theory of McAdams to the postmodern sociological theory of Rose and Foucault, who shift from narrative to *discourse*. The second group of chapters— Knowing Oneself, Controlling Oneself, Caring for Oneself, and (Re)creating Oneself—analyzes some very general interventions to change the self. Although the focus in these chapters is on techniques and methods, I also am interested in the versions of the self being promoted in their use. As a result some of the material dealt with in earlier chapters is applied to an analysis of these techniques and methods. My overall approach is to link theorizations of self and identity with practices for self-formation and change that are advocated in the educational, therapeutic, and popular literature.

A consistent theme in the book is that individuals can be agents in their own formation and change by understanding and acting on the circumstances and forces that surround and shape them. In addition, I argue that those of us involved in education for personal change need to be critical of our own practices and their rationale. And we need to be open to different theoretical ideas and practices, valuing them while at the same time having an irreverent and critical stance toward them.

The reader looking for a systematic treatment of various theories of the self and their educational implications will be disappointed—it is not that type of book. Instead I invite readers to engage critically with theory and then to put *themselves* into practice, rather than putting *theory* into practice (to paraphrase Collins, 1991, p. 47). In this way theory is seen as interacting with practice. Also, I do not subscribe to the view that there is a one-to-one relationship between theory and practice in the sense that a particular teaching method or technique is unique to a particular theory. Rather there are different ways to implement any given method or technique, and embedded within any given implementation are assumptions about the self and its capacity for change. For example, the use and analysis of personal diaries as a method of learning can be done from a psychodynamic, humanistic, critical, social constructionist, or postmodern perspective. It all depends on what type of content is being generated and what type of questions are being asked.

This book has its origins in an article titled "Transforming Selves," which appeared in the *Journal of Transformative Education* (Tennant, 2005). Much of this work was completed while I was a visiting professor at Columbia University, and I thank Professor Victoria Marsick for generously hosting me at Columbia. I also thank my wife, Susie, who has been a constant in my life as a friend, lover, mother to my children, and companion for over thirty-four years.

Sydney, Australia   Mark Tennant
January 2012

About the Author

Mark Tennant is an emeritus professor of education at the University of Technology, Sydney, where he has held the positions of dean of the University Graduate School and dean of the Faculty of Education. His academic focus has been on developing a critical understanding of psychology in its application to pedagogy, with an emphasis on postschool contexts. Mark has published widely and was the recipient of the Cyril O. Houle Award for Literature in Adult Education for his book *Psychology and Adult Learning*. His other books include *Learning and Change in the Adult Years* (with Philip Pogson) and *Teaching, Learning and Research in Higher Education* (with Cathi McMullen and Dan Kaczynski). He has had a number of appointments as a visiting professor in universities in Japan, the United Kingdom, Canada, and the United States. Mark obtained his PhD in psychology from Macquarie University in 1983.

The Learning Self

1

Introduction

A number of features of contemporary life have arguably led to a more intense focus on the self and our capacity to understand, manage, and shape our "selves." We have been increasingly invited to "serve ourselves" as consumers of supermarket products, fuel, banking, travel, entertainment, and even education. Such self-service provisions are supported by rhetoric of personal choice, individual freedom, self-fulfillment, and initiative. In the contemporary workplace too there is a demand for innovative, flexible, multiskilled, and entrepreneurial workers who have a capacity to self-regulate, monitor their performance, be reflexive, and align themselves with the strategic goals of their organization. There are also increasing numbers of independent workers who do not have organizational allegiances but who are conscious of building their portfolio of skills to maintain their position in the labor market—those who can be described as "entrepreneurs of the self" or "portfolio workers" (Gee, 2000). More broadly, rapid social and technological change; the growth of the knowledge society; and global economic, ecological, and health issues collectively point to the need for significant adaptation, flexibility, and a capacity for personal change. One could go further and argue that contemporary life is characterized by uncertainty and dislocation as people find that their anchoring points for identity and their expectations of life trajectories are challenged and disrupted. Clearly, maintaining a singular, unchanging "self" is unlikely to lead to a satisfying and successful life. Instead, we are told, we need to be able to change in response to the changing circumstances in which we find ourselves.

Accepting the idea that we need to undertake significant personal change over our lifetime raises the question of how such change may come about. Can we be the sole agents of our own change? If so, what do we need to think, do, say, or feel to effect this change? If not, to what extent are we dependent on others to effect self-change? What shared activities promote self-change? Is our self-change dependent on change in others? What kinds of relationships with others are necessary for self-change? By changing ourselves, are we able to change our circumstances and those of others? What is the role of the educator or manager in the process of change? (see Tennant, 1998).

Such questions are invariably framed within an explicit or implicit theoretical framework for understanding the self, subjectivity, or identity. One aim of this book is to explore different ways of conceptualizing these terms. This is done by examining some of the key theoretical conceptions of the self, but it is also done by exploring existing techniques, processes, and practices in education, the helping professions, and organizations that are aimed at helping people "work on themselves." Such practices, or "technologies of the self," contain within them assumptions about self and identity and the place of society and culture in personal formation and change.

Ashmore and Jussim (1997) provide a historical overview of the expanding interest in self and identity, from the time of William James's "The Consciousness of Self" (which appears in his seminal work *The Principles of Psychology*, 1890) to the latter part of the twentieth century, during which, from 1974 to 1994, over thirty thousand articles were published on the theme of self and identity in psychology journals alone. Beyond psychology there has been much commentary on self and identity in such diverse fields as sociology, organizational studies, anthropology, cultural studies, and education. A journal dedicated to this theme, the eponymous *Self and Identity*, commenced publication in 2002. As the editors explain, they are attempting to reach a broad, cross-disciplinary audience: "*Self and Identity* will appeal to researchers in sociology, communication, family studies, anthropology, social work, psychiatry, and other social and behavioural sciences as well. Our disciplines have labored too long unaware of or unconcerned with the others, and I hope that the journal can provide a bridge among them" (Leary and Forest, 2002, p. 2).

A similar appeal for interdisciplinary work in this area is made by the editors of the newly named journal *Subjectivity* (which, significantly, is a continuation of the *International Journal of Critical Psychology*):

> *Subjectivity* is an international, transdisciplinary journal that will explore the social, cultural, historical and material processes, dynamics and structures of human experience. As topic, problem and resource, notions of subjectivity are relevant to many disciplines, including cultural studies, sociology, social theory, science and technology studies, geography, anthropology, gender and feminist studies and psychology. The journal will bring together scholars from across the social sciences and the humanities in a collaborative project to identify the processes by which subjectivities are produced, explore subjectivity as a locus of social change, and examine how emerging subjectivities remake our social worlds. Our aim, then, is a re-prioritization of subjectivity as a primary category of social, cultural, psychological, historical and political analysis [Blackman et al., 2008, p. 1].

It is worth noting that both of these journals point to how the three interrelated concepts of self, identity, and subjectivity are deployed in diverse and overlapping ways in psychology, sociology, philosophy, and cultural studies. As the reader may have anticipated, these concepts have not emerged from a singular theoretical perspective or even a singular disciplinary perspective. This chapter comprises an initial exploration of these concepts with a view to understanding the issues each of them signals. I am not providing the reader with a definitive position, but rather a way of exploring different ways we can imagine our "selves," how we are formed and sustained, and the nature of our relationship to others and the broader culture in which we live.

The Self

The dominant image of the self in everyday life and in psychology in particular has been that of a "ghost in the machine" (see Koestler, 1967), which refers to the locus of our experience, thoughts, intentions, actions, and beliefs; it is the inner psychological entity that owns our unique individual biography and our sense of coherence and continuity over time. Although it is probably fair to say that this image underlies much of the theory, research, and practice of psychology (see Allport, 1961; Maslow, 1968; Rogers, 1967), it has not gone unchallenged both within psychology and from without. And psychology certainly cannot lay claim to a monopoly on the topic of the self. Danziger (1997), for example, makes the point that psychologists were relative latecomers to the topic of the self, with the term being in vogue initially in such neighboring disciplinary areas as sociology, philosophy, literary studies, and history. Indeed he points out that the self was a taboo topic in psychology for many decades, especially with the dominance of behaviorism, which rejected, on epistemological grounds, any attempt to uncover inner mental states (see, for example, Skinner's *Beyond Freedom and Dignity*, 1973). Moreover, well before the advent of psychology as a discipline there had emerged, in Western societies at least, specifically psychological ways of thinking about humans and their everyday world. Danziger draws our attention to this by distinguishing between small-"p" psychology and Psychology with a capital "P":

Before there could be anything for the discipline of psychology to study, people had to develop a psychological way of understanding themselves, their conduct, and their experiences. They had to develop specifically psychological concepts and categories for making themselves intelligible to themselves. Only then did aspects of people's lives present themselves as potential objects of psychological study, rather than, say, objects for religious meditation or moral disputation. The history of small-p psychology, therefore, is not the history of primitive "anticipations" of later scientific formulations but the history of the emergence of those discursive objects without which the science of psychology would have had nothing to study [Danziger, 1997, p. 139].

This is a significant claim because it implies that the self is not a natural entity that can be objectively studied. It has a historical rather than a natural status. That is, unlike objects in the physical world, the self is not something that is independent of the way we think, theorize, and talk about it. This claim of course runs counter to much of the early work in the social sciences, which assumed that the self was an object of knowledge that could be known empirically like any other natural phenomenon. Danziger (1997) emphasizes the radical nature of this view at the time when it was first put forward in the philosophical writings of John Locke in *An Essay Concerning Human Understanding* (1694/1959). By considering the self to be an object of knowledge and the source of the unity of the human individual, Locke challenged the hitherto prevailing view that the immortal soul was the key to the unity of the human individual. He was replacing a religious view with a secular view, and this stirred up a sustained controversy (Danziger, p. 141). It opened up the possibility of seeing the self not as sinful and evil but as something positive that can be sustained and nurtured through self-reflection, self-monitoring, and even "self-love." Deviance took on a new angle: it was no longer seen in terms of sinners falling short of divine goodness; instead it was seen as a failure in the monitoring mechanism of the self. This view of the self as having an executive function dominated early-twentieth-century thinking about the self. It is the basis of the idea that the self is composed of the "I," who is the knower, and the "me" or "object," which can be known both by me and by others as a cluster of attributes and actions. This distinction between "I" and "me" is typically attributed to William James's chapter "The Consciousness of Self," which appeared in his seminal work, *Principles of Psychology* (1890). Thus self-evaluation is a matter of the "I," with its executive function, making judgments about the "me," and self-evaluation takes on a moral value: "The objectified self that persons now harbor within them is above all an object of approval and disapproval, both by others and the person herself. The self is always conceived as an object of variable worth, and therefore the desire to raise or maintain its worth comes to be regarded as an identifiable human motive" (Danziger, p. 145).

In therapy and everyday life, self-improvement is now a core cultural value and there exist across the spectrum of human activities numerous practices and procedures that guide individuals to reflect upon and evaluate themselves and their thoughts, feelings, and conduct. Consequently, the vocabulary of self-related constructs and processes has expanded. Leary and Tangney (2003) have tabulated sixty-six "self-" terms employed in over 150,000 PsycInfo abstracts up to June 2001. The most frequent were *self-concept, self-esteem, self-control, self-disclosure, self-actualization, self-monitoring, self-confidence,* and *self-awareness*. For each of these terms there are practices aimed at achieving a normative ideal—it is good to have a stable or realistic concept of oneself, it is good to be self-aware, self-disclosure is a good thing, and so on. Despite the variety of practices, a common normative ideal is the unified, coherent, integrated self. Thus the healthy self is unified rather than split, conscious rather than hidden, and continuous rather than discontinuous with the past.

Identity

Gleason (1983), in documenting the semantic history of identity, observes its ubiquity, elusiveness, and ambiguity. For example, it refers to both *sameness*, as in one's identification with, say, an ethnic group, and *uniqueness*, in the sense that we use the term to describe our particular individual identity. Identity is used to refer to the continuity and unity of the individual over time, but it is also used to refer to multiple and sometimes divided, or at least conflicted, individuals. Gleason distinguishes between the way identity is conceptualized by psychologists such as Erikson (1959), in whose view it is an internal psychological state and a source of continuity in the person, and the way it is understood by sociologists such as Cooley (1922) and Mead (1934/1972), and later Goffman (1971) and Berger (1963), who see identity as socially produced and subject to change with changing circumstances. According to Gleason, "In the case of identity, Erikson insists that an inner continuity of personality endures through all the changes the individual undergoes in passing through the stages of the life cycle, while the interactionists envision a flickering succession of identities adopted and shed according to the requirements of different social situations" (p. 919).

Of particular note is the way the "interactionists" (Cooley and Mead) shifted from an initial use of the term *self* to the term *identity*, perhaps for the reason that it seemed a more promising category with which to explore the relationship between the individual and society. Its use in everyday language also seemed to capture the emerging concerns faced by citizens of Western liberal democracies—at first the concern with how to establish personal identity in an impersonal mass society dominated by the consumption of mass goods; then the concern with how marginalized groups can have their identities recognized and respected in a society dominated by an identity coded as male, white, able-bodied, and heterosexual; and finally the concern with establishing and maintaining an identity in a diverse and ever-changing society. The adoption of identity rather than self as an explanatory category is thus associated with a growing critique of Western liberal democracy, with its mass-produced goods and its norms of conduct. The move to identity thus entails a politicization of the previously "neutral" psychological term *self*. It is also symptomatic of a shift from the private realm of internal states to the public realm of performances in the social world, as depicted by Gee (2000):

> When any human being acts and interacts in a given context, others recognize that person as acting and interacting as a certain "kind of person" or even as several different "kinds" at once. . . . A person might be recognized as being a certain kind of radical feminist, homeless person, overly macho male, "yuppie," street gang member, community activist, academic, kindergarten teacher, "at risk" student, and so on and so forth, through countless possibilities. The "kind of person" one is recognized as "being," at a given time and place, can change from moment to moment in the interaction, can change from context to context, and, of course, can be ambiguous or unstable. Being recognized as a certain "kind of person," in a given context, is what I mean here by "identity." In this sense of the term, all people have multiple identities connected not to their "internal states" but to their performances in society [Gee, p. 99].

Gee goes on to list four ways to view identity: as a state of nature (for example, being an identical twin); as an institutional position (for example, being a bank manager); as a discursive position (for example, being recognized and talked about by others as being a charismatic person); and finally as an affiliation with a group or community with distinctive social practices (for example, being a surfer, a yoga devotee, or a bird watcher). Gee is at pains to point out that these four views are not separate from each other. For example, being an older person may be a state of nature (living to, say, eighty-five years of age); an institutional position (for example, living in an elder-care facility); a discursive position (being recognized and talked about by others as old); and an affiliation (for example, participating in activities for older people). Despite their overlap, these categories help us ask questions about how identities are formed and sustained. To continue the example of older persons, I recall a debate about a catchphrase used to promote Senior Citizens Week in Sydney. The catchphrase originally proposed was, "You are as young as you feel." The objection to this is that it valorizes youth—and it leaves no space for people who actually feel their age to thereby feel good about themselves. The catchphrase was eventually replaced by "Age adds value"—which focuses on the positive aspects of aging without the "youth" tagline. This is a good example of a discursive identity's being resisted and it points to the ways in which discourses compete in fleshing out what it means to be "a certain kind of person." It also points to the role of discourse in forming and sustaining identities.

Although historical usage reveals a significant overlap between the terms *identity* and *self*, the use of identity signals a shift toward the social side of the individual-social dichotomy. From the point of view of individual psychology, *identity* (and its correlate *identification*) are terms that can be harnessed to explain how the social becomes a constituent part of individual psychology. From a social perspective it is clear that identities can be resisted, contested, and negotiated by challenging the interpretive systems underlying them, such as traditions, rules of institutions, social norms, ways of talking about people, and views of what is natural. This is of course recognizable as the terrain of identity

politics, in which marginalized groups seek to have their identities recognized—not tolerated or included—but recognized *as*,
say, women, indigenous people, African Americans, immigrants,
or lesbians. But the language and practices of identity politics, at
least for some, contain remnants of an inner, almost essentialist
self that directs actions and makes choices. The attempt to transform social practices through group and individual "consciousness
raising," and the call for "authenticity" and "self-determination,"
are testimony to this. The shift to subjectivity can be seen partly
as a response to this criticism.

Subjectivity

Blackman et al. (2008) provide an excellent account of the emergence of the term *subjectivity*, with all its dense theoretical twist
and turns. But rather than recount their analysis it is more productive to ask, What problem is being addressed by the shift to
subjectivity? It appears that the problem is the ways in which psychological understandings of the self have dominated academe,
professional psychology, and everyday life for much of the twentieth century. Critics have portrayed psychology as promoting a version of the self as a normative, unitary, coherent, and ahistorical
entity (see, for example, Rose, 1998). They alert us to the political problem with this, namely that such a conception leads to the
portrayal of "acceptable selves" in normative or essentialist terms,
thus disallowing and delegitimizing alternative and minority ways
of being. As Bell (2010) points out, such a conceptualization of
the self was unacceptable to many of the intellectual, social, and
political movements of the twentieth century, such as Marxism,
feminism, antipsychiatry, postcolonialism, and cultural studies:

> The post-war expansion of university education had
> seen huge numbers of hapless humanities students
> respectably schooled in Psychology, albeit an innocently

empirical, eclectically humanistic psychology. The new critics saw in this "science," conformism and intellectual timidity, positivism and political conservatism. . . . [C]onventional psychiatry and psychology, aimed at "adjusting" people to "reality," were increasingly derided. Thomas Szasz, RD Laing, Gregory Bateson, and others agreed with the French critics of psychiatric models of "normality" and opposed the psychiatrically sanctioned control of "patients." Mental illness was a "myth," said Szasz; "asylums" were merely prisons reinforcing the deadening conformity of other institutions like the school and family [Bell, p. 58].

In so far as psychology promotes a "normative" self, it is seen as an instrument of regulation and control, exercising its influence across all spheres of human activity, such as workplaces, schools, prisons, child rearing, sports, health, eldercare, urban living, and the military. It does so by deploying its various techniques to these spheres—most notably psychological tests, questionnaires, or surveys designed to measure such stable, normative psychological characteristics as intelligence, aptitude, personality, attitudes, and values. In this way the discipline and practice of psychology, together with the adoption of psychological ways of thinking in the general population, can be read as providing the basis for people to actively participate in their own subjection. It is worth noting in this respect the highly emotive nature of the critique of psychology and its demonization as the source and primary agent of the "scourges of essentialism, reductionism and dualism" (Blackman et al., 2008, p. 17).

As a normalizing and essentializing practice, psychology has been resisted in two important ways. Politically this resistance took the form of a new celebration of difference and diversity, with the purpose of opening up spaces for previously marginalized and less powerful groups, so that "difference" no longer equated with "deviance" from an established norm. From a scholarly point of view this resistance took the form of a new understanding of the self as *solely* a sociocultural phenomenon—signaled by the use of the term *subjectivity*.

Those who have adopted the term *subjectivity* have in common "the turn to language, signs and discourse as the site through which subjects are formed" (Blackman et al., 2008, p. 3). This represents a shift from analyzing the psychological interior of persons to analyzing the exterior realm of language, signs, and discourses. For example, as Bell (2010) explains, a key approach of cultural studies is to consider cultural phenomena as texts and to deconstruct various texts to unveil the kind of work they do. Texts in this sense can be understood as any cultural phenomena that convey meaning, so that movies, literature, advertising, cooking, music, and of course disciplines, such as psychology, can all be analyzed as texts. The self too is seen as a text—there is no sovereign self, there are only subjects created through discourse. For example, a person can be said to occupy a gendered "subject position," which is sociological and discursive as opposed to psychobiological (see Bell, 2010). According to this view the subject is not to be understood as some kind of entity that stands opposed to the powerful effects of culture; rather it is already one of its effects. Whereas the term *identity* emphasizes the social side of the individual-social dichotomy, the term *subjectivity* dissolves the dichotomy, largely because the individual as such vanishes. The self is pure fiction, and those who attempt to enumerate its qualities are duped into promoting a version of the "truth" that controls and regulates both them and others. Given that the claim to truth is abandoned, it is clear at this point that the key driver behind the analysis of subjectivity is political in nature.

This radical theorization of subjectivity in solely sociocultural terms leads to some significant logical difficulties—not the least of which is the problem of how we come to identify with one socially produced representation and not another (see Bell,

2010, for a more detailed analysis, and Blackman et al., 2008, p. 8). Also, there is the difficulty of accounting for the agency of the subject in resisting control and regulation if the subject is completely constituted in sociocultural terms. For this reason, writers working within this sociocultural tradition now acknowledge the limitations of a purely sociocultural analysis. For example, Blackman et al., with reference to the work of Foucault, ask, "Might we not accept the full significance of Foucault's important arguments concerning the differentiation and production of individuals and not still suggest that the 'subjectivity' of such individuals is not wholly accounted for by power, discourse and historical circumstance?" (p. 9). They answer in the affirmative, arguing that we need to take into account actual bodies and how they modulate and augment subjectivity. They state their case in a rather timid appeal to their would-be critics:

> We are thus emphatically not calling for a return to a naïve individualizing humanism, to de-socialized, a-historical categories of explanation, or to an essentialist inner mechanics of psychological functioning. However, notwithstanding this aversion to de-politicized modes of explanation, to the multiple problems associated with reductive psychological individualism, we remain nevertheless interested in an exploration of those ostensibly psychological frameworks and vernaculars—contingent as they may be—that may enable even a temporary hold on the unique density and complexity of subjectivity which is always more than a derivative formation. There is far more work to be done, for example, in linking the current recourse to affect, central to much contemporary sociological and cultural studies work, with models of psychical or neurological functioning that do not bring in psychological individualism through the back door [Blackman et al., p. 10].

Elizabeth Grosz, in an interview in the *Nordic Journal of Women's Studies*, is more forthright in her disavowal of purely cultural and discursive analysis: "Nature or materiality have no identity in the sense that they are continually changing, continually emerging as new. Once we have a dynamic notion of nature, then culture cannot be seen as that which animates nature. Nature is already animated, and culture borrows its energy from nature. So it is not as if culture is the transformation of nature: culture is the fruition, the culmination of nature. Culture is no longer understood as uniquely human or as a thoroughly linguistic creation" (quoted in Kontturi and Tiainen, 2007, p. 248).

The preceding quotations, from "insiders," so to speak, illustrate that the extreme view of subjectivity as solely a discursive phenomenon has had its day. But there is no doubt that the use of the term has done its work and left its mark, particularly in the way those psychologists who continue to use the term *self* have taken up its historical and discursive dimensions in their theoretical work.

Although there is considerable overlap in the way self, identity, and subjectivity have been used, it is fair to say that the adoption of one term over another tends to signal a particular position on a range of theoretical issues. One issue that is central to the debate is how to conceive of the relationship between the "outside" and the "inside": that is, the relationship between society and the person. An important dimension of this debate is the assumptions that are made about the relative depth and thickness of "human material." Authors du Gay, Evans, and Redman (2000) cite psychoanalysis as having a relatively "thick" view of human material in that it has an elaborate conception of the dynamic "inner" history of the individual that is set against his or her "external" experience of the world. In contrast, theories of subjectivity "presuppose only a minimal or 'thin' conception of the human material on which history operates . . . where the representation of human beings as interiorized and psychologized entities is treated as an historical instance and not as a given" (p. 4).

One's position on this dimension thus serves to demarcate vastly different theoretical positions with vastly different implications for education, therapy, management, and other "interventions in the name of subjectivity" (to borrow a phrase from Rose, 1998, p. 65).

Throughout this book I use the term *self* for pragmatic purposes: to avoid the repetition of the three terms *self*, *identity*, and *subjectivity*, and to admit into the analysis some standard social science approaches that would be denied by the term *subjectivity*. It also signals my interest in how psychological understandings of the self have shifted in response to the critique of those who see such psychological constructions as a form of regulation and control. It also foreshadows a central argument of this book: that individuals can be agents in their own formation by understanding and acting on the circumstances and forces that surround and shape them.

Table 1.1 sets out some of the main ways in which the relationship between self and society has been theorized. It serves to highlight the assumptions we make when we explicitly engage in educational or other interventions in the name of personal change. Broadly speaking, the conceptions of the self in the left-hand column align with the various processes of social impact in the right-hand column, allowing for some crossover.

What are we attempting to do when we intervene in the name of personal change? Are we fundamentally concerned with

Table 1.1   Conceptualizing the Relationship Between Self and Society

Conceptions of the Self	Input of society
Authentic or real self	Distortion
Autonomous self	Shaping
Repressed self	Oppression and domination
Socially constructed self	Discourse
Storied self	Constraining and generating

Source: Adapted from Tennant, 2005.

exposing and undoing the distortions imposed by society? For example, in a typical group learning activity, should we focus on how our participants have developed "false consciousness" or live repressed lives through exposure to oppressive social forces? Are we simply engaged in an exercise to reshape participants' views of themselves and their relationships? Are we encouraging alternative readings of experience so that dominant readings can be challenged? Do we promote the practice of "self-authorship"— creating oneself through narrative? Are we providing a different framework for participants to understand their interpersonal relationships and therefore themselves? And to what end are these interventions aimed? Is there a "real" self to be discovered that has hitherto been buried and hidden from our awareness? Are we content to aim for a less repressed and therefore more conscious self who can engage in life without the debilitating burden of excessive guilt and self-doubt? Are we simply seeking a more autonomous self who can exercise agency and choice through an awareness of and resistance to the forces shaping his or her life? Do we wish to encourage participants to develop coherent, satisfying self-narratives, or perhaps to assist them in understanding the multiple narratives played out in their lives with a view to exploring still further possibilities?

Such questions as these may serve to frame an educational intent, but they can also be used to critically analyze the strategies and practices deployed in the name of learning for change. There is of course a rich history of techniques and practices in religion, philosophy, psychology, and management. All have in common an invitation for people to "act upon themselves" in various ways. Such techniques are explored further in Chapters Seven through Ten under these headings: knowing oneself, controlling oneself, caring for oneself, and (re)creating oneself. Although these categories cut across the various conceptions of self and society examined in earlier chapters, they can be used in combination to critically analyze interventions in the name of the self.

2

The Authentic or Real Self

The concept of an *authentic* or *real* self implies that there is an essence that is you—what has been referred to elsewhere as an "essential" self. The significant thing about an essential self is that it is not changeable; it is the part of you that remains constant with the flux of changing relationships and roles. One view of the essential self is that it is biologically determined through inherited characteristics—characteristics that constitute one's "real" self. This version of the real self presents a particular problem for those in education or the helping professions. First, if it is an accurate portrayal of the real self then any interventions to promote fundamental personal change seem doomed to fail. Second, if such beliefs about the real self are widely held, then irrespective of their legitimacy the beliefs themselves can be a source of resistance to fundamental personal change and need to be challenged. For these reasons those with a professional or personal interest in self-change need to at least explore the biological arguments and develop a position on them.

Another version of the essential self concentrates not on individually inherited characteristics but on our shared characteristics as human beings. The interest here is in how the *authentic* self stands against the *inauthentic* self: how our essential human qualities can be distorted by social forces. The belief is that our true human qualities can be discovered once we shed the distorting and distracting influences of our social and institutional roles. In the search for authenticity these roles are portrayed as distorting or blocking authenticity and so are described in negative terms, such as the "relentless pursuit of material gain" accompanied by long hours of "debilitating and ultimately alienating work." Kreber (2010) points to the long-standing interest in authenticity in Western philosophy from the Greeks to the present day. She also draws our attention to the contemporary interest in authenticity among British and North American academics in the field of adult and higher education (see Barnett, 2006; Walker, 2004; Nixon, 2007). This interest can be related to the growing expectation that education produce among its students the dispositions, personal qualities, and ways of being in the world that allow them to thrive and continue to learn (Barnett, 2006). Barnett goes so far as to assert that "the fundamental educational problem of a changing world is neither one of knowledge nor of skills but is one of *being*. To put it more formally, the educational challenge of a world of uncertainty is ontological in its nature" (p. 51). Educators are thus expected to equip students with the resources for self-formation and self-change—or, if you like, for engineering and reengineering themselves. Academics have drawn on the concept of authenticity to address this challenge. This chapter will examine both of these versions of the essential self: the biological inheritance version and the authenticity version.

Biology and the Self

A popular contemporary trend has been to turn to biology in the pursuit of self-discovery. The mapping of the human genome and advances in neuroscience have arguably prompted a popular interest in biology and a renewed debate concerning the relative effects of nature as opposed to nurture in the formation of human beings (see Pinker, 2002, for a very readable treatment of this issue). A common example of the belief in the biological basis of one's self can be found in those people who search for their "real" (meaning "biological") parents in order to discover who they "really" are. This phenomenon is driven by the contemporary cultural dominance of the equation "biology = real," and thus it is worth exploring.

It is possible to find any number of testimonies to the joy of discovering and meeting one's biological parent(s)—the following, which are extracts from a Web site helping adoptees reunite with their biological parents, being typical:

Exhibit 1

I have just finished spending Easter with my biological family. I discovered I have 2 brothers. I have been accepted with open arms and cannot describe the feeling of being a whole person! Finally, I know who I am. I totally agree with nature vs. nurture. I can put the puzzle pieces together. I love my brothers and hope to be a part of their lives forever. Still on a cloud, Susan ["Adoptee and Birth Parent Reunion Stories," n.d.].

Exhibit 2

If anyone out there is hesitant about searching, don't be. It is the most wonderful feeling finally knowing where you come from. I just wish I had done it sooner. I have a whole other family to add to mine. I'm whole at last! ["Adoptee and Birth Parent Reunion Stories," n.d.].

Exhibit 3

My posting was listed for only a couple of weeks! ! ! I have been searching for my biological mother for 17 years and was found by a first cousin at your web site. I really thought it was never going to happen . . . never . . . never . . . I am still in shock . . . Everyone out there looking please . . . please do not give up! ! ! MY mother went through several marriages (name changes) and moved through several states, I was just about to put the search on the shelf . . . again . . . I am glad

> I didn't one of my three half sisters are coming over
> in about 3 hours . . . I am sooooo nervous and happy.
> Please keep on looking, it's better than winning the
> 25 Million dollar NY lotto drawing (although it would've
> been the icing on the cake)! ! ! ! ["Adoptee and Birth
> Parent Reunion Stories," n.d.].

These testimonies bear witness to the excitement of making contact with biological parents and siblings. They typify the view that nature is more "real" than nurture, as evidenced by the expectation of being "whole at last," the feeling of "knowing where you have come from," and the belief that meeting one's biological parent(s) means that "I know who I am." But of course not every discovery is met with joy, as was evident in the case of Matthew Roberts. As reported in the *Sun* ("I Traced," 2009), Matthew began investigating his family history in 1997 by contacting a social services agency that located his mother, Terry, in Wisconsin. She acknowledged that she was Matthew's biological mother and said she had named him Lawrence Alexander. Terry would not, however, let Matthew know his father's name or whereabouts. After many letters and much cajoling from Matthew, Terry relented and told Matthew his father's name. But nothing could have prepared Matthew for what he was about to discover—that his father was convicted murderer Charles Manson, the infamous sect leader of the Manson Family. Like many others, Terry had been transfixed by Manson, and became a member of his "family." She was eventually raped by Manson, and Matthew was born on March 22, 1968.

Presumably Matthew set out on his quest to find his biological parents with the same beliefs and expectations as those who provided the positive testimonies given earlier. That is, he believed that he was going to discover something about his "true self" and that a new set of relationships might develop with parents and other siblings. Matthew was understandably horrified, especially given his resemblance to Manson. But he did not revise his beliefs about the importance of biology; instead he was perplexed and caught in contradictory emotions: "I didn't want to believe it. I was frightened and angry. It's like finding out that Adolf Hitler is your father. I'm a peaceful person—trapped in the face of a monster. . . . He's my biological father—I can't help but have some kind of emotional connection. That's the hardest thing of all—feeling love for a monster who raped my mother. I don't want to love him, but I don't want to hate him either" ("I Traced," 2009).

The cases cited earlier raise the issue of what insights into the self can be reasonably and legitimately expected from a reunion with biological parents. This issue immediately draws us into one of the most enduring questions in the social and life sciences: What determines our behavior: genes or the environment? It is worth noting that this question itself uses the term *behavior*, not the broader notion of who we are, or our sense of self, which is arguably not reducible to our behavior. The question also sets up a dichotomy between nature and nurture and ignores the interaction of genes and the environment. Finally, the evidence relating to this question comes from a broad range of enquiries into such areas as psychopathology, addiction, personality traits, cognitive development, and intelligence; and it is doubtful whether the balance of genetic versus environmental determinants remains constant across the different areas being investigated, or whether the issue is even applicable across all areas being investigated. Over the years the general debate concerning the relative influence of nature and nurture is typically found in introductory psychology texts; popular science books (for example, Steven Pinker's *The Blank Slate: The Modern Denial of Human Nature*, 2002, and Matt Ridley's *Nature via Nurture: Genes, Experience, and What Makes Us Human*, 2003); and science journalism (for example, Arthur Allen's "Nature and Nurture: When It Comes to Twins, Sometimes It's Hard to Tell the Two Apart," 1998). Much of the very general evidence comes from data obtained from twin studies—the rationale being that identical twins raised apart provide a natural experiment whereby nature (that is, DNA) is controlled and the environment is varied, so that the effects of environmental influences can be separated from inherited characteristics. One of the best-known studies is the Minnesota study of twins reared apart (Bouchard et al., 1990). This longitudinal study gathered data on more than a hundred sets of identical and nonidentical twins (monozygotic and dizygotic), raised together and apart. They were subjected to a range of physical and psychological assessments. The psychological assessments included intelligence tests and multiple measures of personality, temperament, occupational and leisure-time interests, and social attitudes. The researchers concluded that

- Intelligence is strongly affected by genetic factors, accounting for approximately 70 percent of the variation in IQ.
- "On multiple measures of personality and temperament, occupational and leisure-time interests, and social attitudes, monozygotic twins reared apart are about as similar as are monozygotic twins reared together" (p. 223).

On the face of it studies such as this provide compelling evidence of the genetic determinants of behavior. However, there are a number of caveats that need to be applied. The most important of these relates to the independent variable, "experience," which is characterized as either "reared apart" (that is, different experiences) or "reared together" (same experience). This assumes that "reared apart" provides sufficient variation in experience for researchers to monitor its effects. Of particular importance here is that the majority of the participants were from Western countries: the United States, the United Kingdom, Canada, Australia, New Zealand, and West Germany (the only exception being China), and so it could be argued that the twins reared apart and the twins reared together are alike because indeed they have been exposed to *similar* environmental influences! No studies exist comparing identical twins raised in contrasting environments in which there are fundamental differences in language, religion, health, and access to education and work opportunities. The same kind of logic applies to "reared together"—despite being reared together, individuals will still have a history of experiences that are unique to them. Taken as a whole, it is clear that the variation in experience in twin studies is not really measurable in any but the crudest way. A second caveat, somewhat related to the first, concerns how genes operate on the environment. The researchers in the Minnesota study speculate that the genetic determinants of behavior may mediate their effects indirectly through the ways in which the genome *selects* experiences:

> The proximal cause of most psychological variance probably involves learning through experience, just as radical environmentalists have always believed. The effective experiences, however, to an important extent are self-selected, and that selection is guided by the steady pressure of the genome. . . . If this view is correct, the development experiences of monozygotic twins are more similar than those of dizygotic twins, again as environmentalist critics of twin research have contended. . . . [M]onozygotic twins tend to elicit, select, seek out or create very similar effective environments and, to that extent, the impact of these experiences is counted as a genetic influence. . . . [T]he genome impresses itself on the psyche largely by influencing the character, selection, and impact of experiences during development [Bouchard et al., 1990, pp. 227–228].

The argument here is that if the environment allows for a range of experiences, the genetic predispositions of the developing child will influence those experiences. The example the authors give is that children with different temperaments will elicit different parenting responses. Other examples include the gravitation toward activities in which one's natural potential can be realized—such as mathematics for the mathematically talented or music for the musically talented. This is consistent with subsequent views from neuroscience about the plasticity of the brain—meaning that its organization is largely dependent on experience. On this account our innate capacities are only predispositions, say, to learn a language or think about objects and people in certain ways. Our predispositions are "attention grabbers" that ensure we receive "massive experience of certain inputs prior to subsequent learning" (Elman et al., 1996, quoted in Pinker, 2002, p. 84). This of course is an argument for the importance of experience and learning in shaping who we are and how we interact with the world. Pinker mounts an argument against the plasticity thesis. Although he acknowledges that genes must be able to adapt to variations in the physical and social environment, the whole point of this adaptation is to "ensure that despite variable environments, a *constant* organ develops, one that is capable of doing its job" (p. 90). But Pinker seems to overlook an important interpretation of plasticity, at least from a social science perspective. As Pinker acknowledges, "A gene cannot anticipate every detail of the environment" (p. 90). But from a social science perspective it is the details that count. That organs or genes remain constant and do their job is not the point—the point is that the results of their work can differ so markedly. This is the terrain of social science, the most obvious example being the acquisition of language. We certainly have a genetic potential to learn a language, but it would be absurd to consider that there is a gene for each and every language that exists. Although language in the abstract may have biological determinants, specific languages are social artifacts. By extension we could list many aspects of being human that are beyond the reach of specific genes—a *particular* religion being one example. What could we include in or exclude from this list? A general principle would be to include any human characteristic that is not universally present across cultures on the grounds that it must either be learned in some cultures and not in others or suppressed in some cultures and not in others—either way the environment is present as a determining factor. Specific beliefs, attitudes, and values are the most obvious, but would we include personality traits, such as those in the Minnesota twin study? Bouchard and Loehlin (2001) would clearly exclude personality traits: "Enough empirical evidence . . . has now been gathered to convince anyone but the most extreme skeptic that virtually all human psychological traits are influenced by genetic factors to a significant degree. The primary consequence of this finding is that much contemporary social science research is uninterpretable if it does not incorporate the influence of genetic variation into its explanatory models" (p. 243).

Bouchard and Loehlin then go on to cite evidence of the genetic determinants of personality traits from nonhuman animal studies of personality together with other evidence including that gathered in the twin studies. Despite this evidence, the problem of measuring personality traits remains. The authors themselves point out the great variation in the ways in which personality traits are conceived and measured. Much of the research in behavioral genetics has relied on Eysenck's three global traits—extraversion, neuroticism, and psychoticism (1960). But there are competing models, such as that of McCrae and Costa (1997), which includes the traits of extraversion, neuroticism, agreeableness, conscientiousness, and openness, and others proposed by Tellegen (1985) and Zuckerman and Cloninger (1996). Despite their similarities, these competing models are based on different conceptions of these traits, and although they may be aiming to get at something more fundamental they are in fact competing constructions, and it is hard to see how this can ever be resolved. One does not have to be very skeptical to question whether there could be an "agreeableness" or "openness" gene, especially given the highly value-laden and culturally relative nature of these concepts.

One further point needs to be made on this debate, and it concerns the role of learning. Even the most ardent proponents of the genetic determinants of behavior will acknowledge the important role of learning. But there is a curious logic about how they represent learning. First, they argue, learning is a by-product of our genetic makeup, which determines our capacities and proclivities for learning particular things. Second, and seemingly following on from the first point, an incapacity to learn or unlearn something is offered as evidence of a genetic determinant. This is well illustrated in the following passage from Pinker (2002), who comments on sexual orientation: "Most gay men feel stirrings of attraction to other males around the time of the first hormonal changes that presage puberty. . . . In the less tolerant past, unhappy gay men sometimes approached psychiatrists for help in changing their sexual orientation. . . . Many techniques have been foisted upon them: psychoanalysis, guilt mongering, and conditioning techniques that use impeccable fire-together-wire-together logic (for example, having them look at Playboy centre-folds while sexually aroused). The techniques are all failures . . . the sexual orientation of most gay men cannot be reversed by experience. Some parts of the mind just aren't plastic" (p. 94).

I am interested in the logic of this argument rather than its truth or otherwise, and the logic is flawed. Pinker seems to think that what cannot be learned, or unlearned in this case, must therefore be part of our genetic blueprint. However, there are many things that we have learned in the past that are resistant to unlearning. Language is an example again—apart from a brain injury, it is difficult to imagine a circumstance in which a language can be completely unlearned once it is fully developed (especially if you only have one language!). The same is true of our understanding of concepts, such as number (can you imagine unlearning the addition of $2 + 2 = 4$?), and is at least partially the case with a host of skills, such as playing a musical instrument or riding a bike. Certainly some capacities, once they are learned, become "hardwired," but this does not mean that they were not learned in the first instance. On this question of the hardwiring of the brain, it is worth noting the remarks of Evan Balaban (2006), a neuroscientist from the Behavioral Neurosciences Program at McGill University, who points to the importance of random events in the brain. Commenting on the area of cognitive development, he notes that the role of biology is typically seen deterministically. He points to the indeterminacy of the organization of the brain, whether this organization is shaped through genetic influences or through experience: "Biologically based thinking about cognitive development has formerly put too much emphasis on organizational effects (both experientially mediated and independent of experience), and too little emphasis on probabilistic factors that importantly influence the functional characteristics of behavioral circuitry" (p. 327).

I began this excursion into the nature-nurture debate as an attempt to understand what we could legitimately expect to learn about ourselves from a reunion with a previously unknown birth parent. Our genetic makeup is clearly relevant to such things as our appearance, our health, some mannerisms, some talents, a proportion of our cognitive capacity, some predispositions—but although this is significant, it does not seem to have a bearing on who we are, what we have become. Ultimately the "biology = real" equation is not a route to the "real, authentic me." Our very particular way of being in the world is the result of a unique set of experiences—what we are is what we have learned to be, and for the most part this can be changed. Having said this, I am not advocating the view that the self is solely the product of language, society, and culture. It is clear that our experiences work on our basic biological material, but, as Grosz argues in a published interview (see Kontturi and Tiainen, 2007), it is important to understand biology as dynamic and open-ended and not fixed and ahistorical. Thus it is possible to acknowledge the biological roots of the self without positing an essential, fixed self (see Hunt and West, 2009).

Living an Authentic Life

There has been a long-standing concern in the social sciences with the phenomenon of alienation—the idea that we can become alienated from what we truly are as human beings. A key influence in shaping this notion in the development of the social sciences in the twentieth century can be found in Karl Marx's *The Economic and Philosophical Manuscripts* (1932/1993), in which Marx writes about estranged or alienated labor. He argues that, under capitalism, workers become alienated from the objects they produce and from their own nature in the process of work: "The object that labor produces, its product, stands opposed to it as *something alien*, as a power independent of the producer. The product of labor is labor embodied and made material in an object, it is the *objectification* of labor. . . . The worker therefore only feels himself outside his work, and in his work feels outside himself. He feels at home when he is not working, and when he is working he does not feel at home. . . . [S]o is the worker's activity not his spontaneous activity. It belongs to another; it is the loss of his self" (pp. 2–4).

Marx was writing in 1844, when the conditions of work following the Industrial Revolution were particularly alienating, but his argument resonates with much contemporary commentary on current work practices. Underlying Marx's analysis is a dynamic psychology based on the individual's relatedness to the world, to others, and to nature. He recognizes that particular social and economic conditions can create appetites, drives, and needs that are not human and therefore alienating. These are distinct from the constant or fixed drives, such as the need for sex, for food, and for relatedness to others and to nature. In his essay "Marx's Contribution to the Knowledge of Man," Fromm (1973) writes: "The question how to distinguish between human and inhuman, real and imaginary, helpful and poisonous needs is, indeed, a fundamental psychological problem that neither psychology nor

Freudian psychoanalysis could even begin to investigate. . . . [H]ow could they make such distinctions when their model is the alienated man, when the fact that modern industry creates and satisfies more and more needs is taken as a sign of progress and when the contemporary concept of freedom, to a large extent, reflects the freedom of the customer to choose between various and virtually identical brands of the same commodity . . . ?" (pp. 78–79).

Much has been written in the late twentieth and early twenty-first centuries about the alienating impact of mindless consumerism. The argument is that with the loss of family, community, tradition, and some degree of certainty in one's life trajectory, the self becomes empty, and is filled by consuming goods, experiences, food, services, personal relationships, and even education (see Cushman, 1990, for a psychological analysis of this issue). Instead of having a life, we now have a lifestyle. The human condition has for some time now been one of inauthenticity, largely because contemporary economic and social conditions have created needs that work against our nature and against living authentically. The problem set out by Fromm remains: How do we distinguish between authentic and inauthentic needs? Anyone making this distinction will need to provide a justifiable view of human nature, and perhaps develop an ethical and ultimately political stance on how we "ought" to be. This issue is particularly salient for teachers and others in the helping professions, in which authenticity is actively promoted and highly valued as an ideal. The concept of authenticity therefore deserves our attention.

Ashton (2010) perhaps best expresses what is meant by authentic "being in the world" (p. 10):

- Remaining properly aware of ourselves, people, other inhabitants of the world and our relations with them
- Being prepared to choose and act independently in sustaining authentic being, including risking, and bearing

the consequences of standing out from the crowd as who and what we are

- Taking responsibility for our lives and what we choose to do, say, think, feel, believe, and value

- Accepting that to choose authenticity or inauthenticity is to choose a basic way of being-in-the-world

- Care for Being—living and non-living, including the physical world that we share

These qualities are echoed in Kreber et al.'s analysis (2007) of the literature on conceptions of authenticity in teaching. Their exhaustive review maps out the range of ideas and values associated with authenticity in teaching: emphasizing the person as a whole (which may include references to integrity, identity, and spirituality); being conscious of self, others, and one's relationships and context; being candid about beliefs, values, and prejudices; confronting the truth about oneself; being more conscious, more individuated; caring about the subject and the students; merging self and teacher; working toward congruence of values and actions; and promoting authenticity in others. It is important for them that authenticity involve "confronting the truth, opening oneself up to one's own limited possibilities, not being defined by social norms, and not clinging to comfortable routines" (Kreber et al., p. 31).

With reference to the work of Baxter Magolda (2001), they argue that "to meet the challenges of our times, students need to develop *self-authorship*, an intellectual, moral, and personal complexity that undergirds their readiness for coping with the multiple personal, vocational, and civic challenges they encounter after college" (Kreber et al., 2007, p. 30). They equate this idea of self-authorship with authenticity and draw a connection with the notions of being an authentic teacher and fostering authenticity among learners. Baxter Magolda (1998, 2001) herself outlines three principles of teaching that promote self-authorship among students:

- Learners are seen as "knowers."
- Learning is situated within learners' experiences.
- Learning is conceptualized as mutually constructing knowledge.

An authentic learning environment, then, is one in which there is openness, trust, caring, and critical reflection on the self and others by both teachers and learners—an environment in which learners and teachers are wholly engaged in meaningful learning activities. This of course is an ideal worth striving for but never realized in practice, largely because the process of teaching and learning necessarily involves participants with different needs, interests, and sources of power. Prominent educator Stephen Brookfield (2006), although endorsing authenticity as an ideal, is mindful of the dynamic of power at play. After outlining his views on the indicators of authenticity, such as congruence between words and actions, full disclosure of expectations and assumptions, responsiveness, and the involvement of one's whole self in the classroom, Brookfield alerts us to a dilemma by posing the question, "How do we exercise power in an ethical and responsible manner while being authentic?" (p. 11), to which he replies:

> We must never confuse responsiveness with capitulation to majority wishes or always doing what students say they want. Instead, we must understand responsiveness as fully addressing learners' concerns and questions, even if this means rejustifying why we can't do what they say they want us to do. In this situation, being responsive is to explain as fully and convincingly as possible why you believe sticking to your agenda is in their

best long-term interests, even if they violently disagree with your position. Of course, this is much easier said than done, and there are often strong personal, institutional, and professional pressures to teach in a way that pleases students [Brookfield, 2006, p. 14].

Brookfield thus alerts us to the complexity and difficulty of adhering to just one characteristic of authentic teaching: responsiveness. The issue has to do with the distinction between wants and needs and who is in the best position to judge the difference. This goes to the heart of the critical theorists' critique of authenticity, that it is not possible just to look inwardly for authenticity without a consideration of how our consciousness is historically shaped through the workings of ideology (see Kreber et al., 2007, p. 34). In a teaching and learning context this means that learners are not necessarily in the best position to know their needs. Of course teachers' subject knowledge also comes into play here, and this is the basis of their authority to judge what is in the best interests of learners. But once again this is complex, especially given that teachers are often institutionally and professionally socialized such that they become agents of socialization into everyday ways of being in the profession, supporting existing practices, values, and attitudes of a particular profession or discipline. Furthermore, teachers are likely to have been socialized into largely accepting dominant cultural and social values, and may not always be open to the diversity the learners bring to the classroom. This is precisely why authentic teaching must necessarily embrace a critical approach, with teachers adopting a critical posture toward themselves and their world, while at the same time encouraging a critical approach among learners. Without such a critical approach it is likely that the characteristics of authentic teaching will be given only lip service and that teachers will fall into the traps that Brookfield (2006) identifies: "spuriously democratic teachers," "counterfeit critical thinkers," and "phony responsiveness" (p. 7).

If we agree with Barnett's assertion (2006) that the educational problem today is one of "being," then teachers of all kinds certainly have a responsibility to promote authenticity among learners so they can lead meaningful, authentic lives in their respective communities and workplaces. This does not mean a rejection of established practices, norms, and values, but it does require a preparedness to question them, and some insight into how such practices, values, and norms were historically produced and whose interests they serve.

3

The Autonomous Self

The autonomous self is characterized by agency, choice, reflection, and rationality. It stands in contrast to the automaton, who simply acts out prescribed behaviors and social roles without any sense of agency or choice, as if he or she were simply shaped or conditioned by social forces. The idea of personal autonomy as a route to psychological health and happiness has mainly been promulgated by humanistic psychologists. It is closely associated with the concept of authenticity, but it differs in important respects, the emphasis being on self-sufficiency, independence, practical judgment, action, self-control, and self-mastery rather than on the discovery and expression of one's "real," authentic self. In addition, it would be wrong to see society as distorting our "true" autonomous nature. Rather society shapes and regulates our beliefs and actions, and we are complicit to the extent that we fall into a complacent world of conformity and fail to analyze and reflect on our beliefs and actions. The idea of autonomy has a long history as an ideal in Western thought, and consequently it has been adopted as an important aim of education—particularly liberal education. It also underpins a dominant ethos in adult teaching and learning: the idea of the self-directed learner. This chapter commences by considering the meanings given to autonomy both as a political goal and as a psychological attribute and marker of psychological health. I then take up some of the educational claims for autonomy as an important goal and a means of personal empowerment.

The Nature of Autonomy

As a starting point it is worthwhile noting the various dimensions of autonomy and how they interact: the political dimension, the emotional dimension, and the intellectual dimension. The political dimension has to do with self-governance. When applied to nation-states, autonomy is the freedom and independence to make laws and govern the country without external coercion. Within a liberal democracy it is the separation of powers—the independence and freedom of the executive, the judiciary, and the legislature. At the personal level, self-governance typically refers to the freedom to choose and act without external coercion. In the case of children, it is fairly clear that parents constrain their political freedom, directing their choices on a range of everyday matters, such as what to wear, what to eat, and what kind of activities to engage in and their timing. It is also pretty clear that parents want to give their children more political freedom as they mature, so that negotiation replaces unilateral parental direction and self-control replaces coercion.

A normative goal of parenting is thus to foster in children the capacity to make responsible, independent choices in life. This political autonomy, however, is closely tied to parents' perception of their children's emotional and intellectual autonomy. No wonder then that emotional and intellectual autonomy are also considered important developmental goals, and that they are defining attributes of mature adulthood. Emotional autonomy has to do with self-mastery, self-discipline, self-sufficiency, perhaps a certain psychological or emotional detachment, being conscious of one's feelings and inclinations, and a capacity to act on one's decisions while remaining focused and not being diverted by whims and impulses (see Gibbs, 1979; Crittenden, 1978). Intellectual autonomy has to do with the capacity to have independent thoughts and make independent judgments—judgments based not on authority but on experience, evidence, and argument. It refers to the ability to bring critical and rational reflection to bear on an issue without bias or prejudice.

Having acknowledged these various dimensions of autonomy, it remains to note how they are interdependent and overlap. For example, within a liberal democracy the concept of autonomy also pervades key institutions and practices, largely to protect personal autonomy: we see it operating through the principle of informed consent in research and medical ethics, in privacy legislation, in the protection of free speech, and in social legislation that aims to provide minimum resources to support the capacity of individuals to choose freely (see May, 1994). The classical liberal concern has been with the freedom to choose without interference.

Many of the debates about legislation aimed at preserving individual choice have centered on the identification of who is doing the interfering or, to put it another way, who has the right to choose. For example, legislation prohibiting smoking in public transportation and then in public places is based on the idea of the freedom of nonsmokers to breathe fresh air without the interference of smokers who otherwise constrain this freedom. It is not surprising that the counterclaim from the smoking lobby concerns the freedom of smokers to smoke without the interference of the law. There are many other examples of legislation, enacted or proposed, that stimulate debate, largely because one group's free choice constitutes another's constraint on choice—the most long-standing and divisive of these debates being the issue of abortion legislation, but the most contemporary example being the wearing of the burka among Muslim women. Opposing camps in such debates are frequently driven by entrenched beliefs and values that are rarely questioned. It is worth noting here that critics of liberalism have pointed to its failure to recognize the power of social forces to shape individual subjective needs, wants, and preferences. They argue that liberalism pays insufficient attention to the ways in which individuals can be impelled or constrained by beliefs, attitudes, values, and ideologies that are internalized as part of their psychological structure.

To expand on the issue of the burka by way of illustration, it is often cited as an example of women's oppression, but those who wear the burka argue against proposals to ban it (hypothetical or otherwise) on the grounds of individual choice and freedom or on the grounds that such a ban would be contrary to the plural traditions of Western democracy and would constitute discrimination (and therefore oppression) of a particular religious group. If we accept the idea of oppressed people acting as agents of their own oppression, then we could argue that those who wear the burka are not exercising free choice in the sense that they are compelled by their belief system and that despite their protestations to the contrary they are perpetuating their own and other women's domination by men. But of course such a reading of the situation would need to be supported by evidence and argument that the burka does in fact symbolize oppression. For example, take the observation that for many women in the world failure to wear the burka would lead to some kind of punishment: in such instances the claim of free choice could not be sustained in the absence of legitimate alternatives for these women. Of course this would never justify a ban on the burka, it would only justify programs to engage burka-clad women in reflecting critically on their situation. There is a parallel here with second-wave feminism in the 1970s with respect to the traditional role of women in the workplace and the community, which among other things led to "consciousness-raising" groups being formed to challenge prevailing norms. Understandably such interventions are seen by some as patronizing or, worse still, oppressive. The emphasis now placed on the values of diversity and difference has somewhat muddied the waters when it comes to intervening in the lives of others in name of raising consciousness or promoting critical awareness. Indeed the very concepts of autonomy and choice have been portrayed by some commentators as an essential part of a regulatory regime whereby we come to govern ourselves in keeping with contemporary political and economic circumstances: "The self-steering capacities of individuals are now construed as vital resources for achieving private profit, public tranquillity, and social progress, and interventions in these areas have also come to be guided by the regulatory norm of the autonomous, responsible subject, obliged to make its life meaningful through acts of choice" (Rose, 1998, p. 160).

Such claims need to be taken seriously and addressed by those working in education and the helping professions. For the present purpose it is sufficient to note that autonomy as an ideal state would need to include the formation of beliefs, values, and principles that are not ready-made but rather the result of ongoing evaluation and critique:

> It is necessary for his autonomy that a person be capable of rational choice, and for that he needs criteria and a conceptual scheme for grasping the issues. How could he come by them unless he learnt them in the first instance from the people about him? Someone not so equipped would not be free, able to make anything of himself; he would be able to make nothing of himself, hardly a person at all. To be autonomous one must have reasons for acting, and be capable of second thoughts in the light of new reasons; it is not to have a capacity for conjuring criteria out of nowhere.
>
> Within this conception of a socialized individual, there is room to distinguish one who simply accepts the roles society thrusts on him, uncritically internalizing the received mores, from someone committed to a critical and creative conscious search for coherence. The autonomous man does not rest on the unexamined if fashionable conventions of his sub-culture when they lead to palpable inconsistencies. He will appraise one

aspect of his tradition by critical canons derived from
another [Benn, 1976, p. 126].

This is the paradox of autonomy: if it can only be realized within
the socialization practices of a particular sociocultural tradition,
how can we distinguish between beliefs and values that are "one's
own" and those that are generated by others and adopted uncriti-
cally as "one's own"? The key is the capacity to be critical; the
conditions for the emergence of personal autonomy are simply the
freedom to think and act in the world and the encouragement to
critically analyze one's own and others' beliefs and actions.

I have just set out some of the things that need to be considered when autonomy is proffered as an educational and developmental goal—the different dimensions of autonomy and their
interdependence; the centrality of autonomy in the operation
of liberal democratic societies; the various ways in which autonomy, and therefore our choices, are constrained by both external
and internal forces; and the different theoretical perspectives on
autonomy, namely the humanistic and critical.

Autonomy as a Psychological Attribute

I would now like to turn to some of the psychological literature
on autonomy. Critics, such as Rose (1998), who argue that psychology is a discipline and practice that serves to regulate our
existence, typically sketch psychology as a humorist would sketch
a cartoon—a caricature portrait that leaves out the detail and the
subtleties. An early critical account of psychological constructs is
that of Gilligan (1986), who argued that separateness, autonomy,
and independence are essentially male values, and that females
value relationships and responsibilities, empathy and attachment,
and interdependence rather than independence. Whereas the
identity of boys is built upon contrast and separateness from their
primary caregiver (invariably female), the identity of girls is built

on the perception of sameness and attachment to their primary caregiver:

> Since masculinity is defined through separation while femininity is defined through attachment, male gender identity is threatened by intimacy, while female gender identity is threatened by separation. Thus males tend to have difficulty with relationships, while females tend to have problems with individuation. The quality of embeddedness in social interaction and personal relationships that characterises women's lives in contrast to men's, however, becomes not only a descriptive difference but also a developmental liability when the milestones of childhood and adolescent development in the psychological literature are markers of increasing separation. Women's failure to separate then becomes by definition a failure to develop [Gilligan, 1986, p. 9].

Gilligan's argument is that womanhood is rarely equated with mature, healthy adulthood in much of the developmental literature. This is because the idea of the healthy, developed personality is predominantly portrayed from a male perspective. Gilligan was responding to well-known contemporary works that described psychological development using such terms as *individuation* (Levinson, 1978, 1996) and *autonomous stage* (Loevinger, 1976). These original works are still cited in contemporary psychology texts, so a closer look at the theoretical context in which these terms are deployed is warranted.

In his early study, Levinson (1978) focused on the decade of thirty-five to forty-five years old, the period representing a shift from youth to middle age. Using a sample of only forty subjects, his approach was to study each person intensively and examine his life in detail. He only studied men, partly because he was interested in his own psychological development as a male, and partly because he was conscious of the psychological differences between men and women. His sample comprised four occupational subgroups of ten men each: ten hourly workers from two companies, ten executives from two companies, ten academic biologists from two universities, and ten novelists who had published at least two books. He focused on working life because he believed that work is of central psychological importance for the self. The sample was deliberately diverse, being made up of people from different social classes, racial-ethnic-religious origins, and educational attainment backgrounds (Levinson, 1978). Levinson described his research method as follows: "A biographical interview combines aspects of a research interview, a clinical interview and a conversation between friends. . . . Our essential method was to elicit the life stories of forty men, to construct biographies and to develop generalizations based upon these biographies. . . . In each case we began by immersing ourselves in the interview material and working toward an intuitive understanding of the man and his life. Gradually we tried more interpretive formulations and, going back and forth between the interviews and the analysis, came to a construction of the life course" (pp. 15–16). Levinson became aware that his biographical approach yielded data on the earlier years of the lives of these men. He was thus retrospectively investigating not only the years thirty-five to forty-five but also the period from entry into adulthood until the late forties.

Levinson (1996) has since published a study of the lives of forty-five women. He once again used intensive biographical interviewing, this time with a sample comprising forty-five women: fifteen "homemakers" and thirty "career women," the latter divided into "businesswomen" and "academics." Despite finding important gender differences in life circumstances and the life-course, and in ways of going through each developmental period (Levinson, 1996), Levinson adhered to his general theoretical framework developed in relation to his study of men.

Levinson's description (1978) of the life cycle is straightforward: it is made up of a sequence of four eras, the duration of each being approximately twenty-five years. He identifies a number of developmental periods within these eras, with a particular emphasis on early and middle adulthood. For example, early adulthood is from the ages of seventeen to forty-five and is characterized by the developmental periods of "early adult transition," "entering the adult world," "age thirty transition," and "settling down." Middle adulthood is from forty-five to sixty and contains the periods of "midlife transition," "entering middle adulthood," "age fifty transition," and "culmination of middle adulthood."

Levinson considers each era to have a distinct and unifying character of living. Thus the transition between eras signals a basic change in the character of one's life, which may take between three and six years to complete. Within these broad eras are periods of development. A period is characterized by a set of tasks that need to be completed and the broader attempt to build or modify one's life structure. For example, in the early adult transition period the two primary tasks are to move out of the preadult world and to make preliminary steps into the adult world. Similarly, the settling down period involves undertaking the task of establishing a niche in society and working toward progress and advancement in that niche. Levinson refers to the "Dream" as a pervasive theme throughout the various periods. The Dream is the imagined possibility in one's life—a vision for oneself that generates excitement and vitality. It is our conception of the ideal life. Throughout the lifecourse the place and nature of the Dream in one's life are constantly modified and revisited as the imagined self is compared with the world as it is lived.

Levinson's concept of *individuation* refers to another fundamental process occurring throughout the life cycle. Individuation commences with the child's dawning knowledge of his or her separate existence in a world of animate and inanimate objects. This marks the beginning of an ever-changing relationship between the self and the external world throughout the lifecourse. In the early adult transition period, the reappraisal and modification of relationships with family and significant others are apparent. Significantly, much of developmental progress can be seen in terms of the changing nature of the relationships between self and others, such as love and family relationships, mentoring relationships, and occupational relationships. The reappraisal of relationships in midlife takes the form of a struggle between the polarities of attachment and separateness: "We use the term 'attachment' in the broadest sense, in order to encompass all the forces that connect person and environment. To be attached is to be engaged, involved, needy, plugged in, seeking, rooted. . . . At the opposite pole is separateness. This is not the same thing as isolation or aloneness. A person is separate when he is primarily involved in his inner world—a world of imagination, fantasy, play. His main interest is not in adapting to the 'real world' but in constructing and exploring an imagined world, the enclosed world of his inner self" (Levinson, 1978, p. 239).

Levinson viewed midlife as a period in which there is a need to redress the dominance of attachment to the external world: to find a better balance between the needs of the self and the needs of society—a greater integration of the poles of separateness and attachment. "Greater individuation allows [a person] to be more separate from the world, to be more independent and self-generating. But it also gives a person the confidence and understanding to have more intense attachments in the world and to feel more fully a part of it" (Levinson, 1978, p. 195).

So individuation is one of the processes that fosters the development of relationships. In this sense it is paradoxical—it points to a developmental move away from the world, but this independence and separateness function to make the person part of the world. Individuation is also apparent in the attempt to integrate polarities within the self, such as the polarities of masculine and feminine, young and old, destructive and creative. Thus individuation serves to integrate previously separated aspects of the self, such as the feminine in men and the masculine in women. Levinson (1978) comments on the inability of an excessively masculine man to form a relationship with a woman: "He does not wish to know any woman well because he is afraid to know himself well—especially the less masculine aspects of himself" (p. 235). A closer reading of Levinson, then, reveals a theoretical sensitivity to the importance of relationships in development—that a strong sense of self and others, which he calls individuation, is necessary for the formation of mature adult relationships.

This is also true for Loevinger (1976), who describes a number of stages of ego development. She takes pains not to link them to specific ages, even though they are age related. For example, the symbiotic and impulsive states are clearly those of infancy, when there is the beginning of the differentiation of self and nonself and an impulsive assertion of one's separate identity. Loevinger's stages are described in terms of impulse control, interpersonal style, conscious preoccupations, and cognitive style. For example, the "Conformist Stage" is characterized by a conformity to external rules (impulse control), a sense of belonging and superficial niceness (interpersonal style), a conscious preoccupation with appearance and social acceptability, and a cognitive style based on stereotypes and clichés. It is noteworthy that the "Autonomous Stage" follows on from the "Individualistic Stage," thus differentiating it from the heightened sense of individuality and concern with dependency that characterize the Individualistic Stage: "The Autonomous Stage is so named partly because the person at that point recognizes other people's need for autonomy. . . . The Autonomous person, however, typically recognizes the limitations of autonomy, that emotional interdependence is inevitable. He will often cherish personal ties as among his most precious values" (Loevinger, p. 23).

In a manner similar to that of Levinson, Loevinger conceives of autonomy in terms of relatedness and interdependence.

I should emphasize that this tension between individuation-separateness-autonomy and connectedness-relatedness is one that is ongoing in psychology. Kagitcibasi (2005) refers to the contemporary emphasis on both the importance and compatibility of autonomy and relatedness. Citing research on adolescence, a period during which issues of autonomy and relatedness are played out, he concludes that "close ties and attachment to parents, rather than detachment, is associated with adolescent health and well-being in diverse cultures. . . . [S]imilarly research . . . also points to the positive association between autonomous (i.e., secure) attachment and positive relationships with parents . . . thus integrating autonomy with relatedness rather than with separateness" (p. 406). He questions why the main developmental task of adolescence continues to be labeled "separation-individuation" when it actually encompasses relatedness and connectedness. He concludes that it is because psychology has an individualistic worldview and is therefore biased toward individualistic rather than collectivist labels. But this does not invalidate the rather paradoxical link between autonomy and relatedness in psychological theory and practice.

Promoting Autonomy Among Learners

From the point of view of those who are interested in promoting autonomy as an important and valued attribute, there appear to be three fundamental approaches one can take: the humanistic, the liberal, or the critical approach.

The humanistic approach is exemplified by Carl Rogers. Rogers was a clinical psychologist who was primarily concerned with improving the psychological health of his clients. It is to be expected, then, that the educational practices he advocates are adapted from his clinical or therapeutic techniques. Rogers's conception (1983) of the teacher as a *facilitator of learning* is testimony to this, as can be seen from the way he describes the qualities of a good facilitator:

1. *Realness and genuineness:* "When the facilitator is a real person, being what she is, entering into a relationship with the learner without presenting a front or façade, she is much more likely to be effective. . . . It means that she is *being* herself, not denying herself" (pp. 121–122).

2. *Prizing, acceptance, and trust:* "Think of it as prizing the learner, prizing her feelings, her opinions, her person. It is a caring for the learner. But a non-possessive caring. It is an acceptance of this other individual as a separate person, having worth in her own right. It is a basic trust—a belief that this other person is somehow fundamentally trustworthy" (p. 124).

3. *Empathic understanding:* "[This is] the ability to understand the student's reactions from the inside . . . a sensitive awareness of the way the process of education and learning seems to the student" (p. 129).

Rogers accepts the learner's view of the world as a starting point for learning; the learner's autonomy is, in effect, a pre-given state. The driver of learning is the learner's natural tendency to self-actualize, and thus the facilitator occupies a neutral position. In Rogers's view, being a good "facilitator" of learning means having empathy with and trust in learners; being genuine with learners; and being open, caring, and nonjudgmental. And so "learner-centered" education is characterized by a focus on developing a good teacher-learner relationship in an attempt to understand and meet learners' needs. As Pratt and Nesbit (2000) comment: "This was an important discursive shift. . . . Now content, and the specification of what was to be learned, was subordinate to the learner's experience and participation. . . . Learners were to be involved in specifying what would be learned, how it would be learned, and what would be an appropriate indication of learning. . . . The learner's experience, as a form of foundational knowledge, replaced the teacher's expertise as the primary compass that guided learning. As a consequence, the primary role of teacher shifted from teacher-as-authority to teacher-as-facilitator" (p. 120).

This view of learning was taken up in the adult learning literature, with Knowles's promulgation (1978) of the idea of self-directed learning. He argued that teachers of adults should use techniques that build upon adults' natural capacity and desire to plan and conduct their own learning. This means that the role of the teacher becomes that of a facilitator of learning—of one who assists learners in formulating goals and objectives, locating appropriate resources, planning learning strategies, and evaluating the outcomes of learning. Thus self-directed learning is characterized by the mastery of a set of techniques and procedures for learning, and the role of the teacher is to help students "learn how to learn." In a group situation the tension in this approach has always been how best to manage the seemingly irreconcilable needs of the group with those of the individuals who make up the group. Every group at some stage infringes on individual autonomy, and therefore a judgment must be made about the relative importance of group as opposed to individual autonomy. This judgment invariably raises issues of power and control, which means that group learning becomes a political site. But such issues are not dealt with in the humanistic approach. Humanistic educators, such as Knowles, have been justly criticized for being too technical and for ignoring both the content (that is, the subject matter) and context of learning.

The liberal tradition is highly focused on content. Although it endorses educational outcomes very similar to those of the humanistic tradition in that it seeks to promote among learners a greater awareness of self and the cultivation of an identity that is independent, rational, autonomous, and coherent and that includes a sense of social responsibility, it advocates a very different route to these outcomes. The good learner is one who, with proper guidance, is brought to apprehend "the great outlines of knowledge, the principles on which it rests, the scale of its parts, its lights and shades. . . . [H]ence it is that his education is called 'Liberal.' A habit of mind is formed which lasts through life, of which the attributes are freedom, equitableness, calmness, moderation and wisdom" (Newman, 1999, p. 93).

In the liberal tradition the subject of pedagogy is the production of a singular ideal type—the "educated person"—toward which one progressively develops through disciplined study and engagement in rational argument. Engaging in disciplined study, of course, means both self-discipline and studying the subject matter and approaches of a particular discipline. It therefore promotes "subject matter autonomy" rather than "general autonomy as a learner." Thus the exemplar of the autonomous learner is the person who has developed a critical capacity in a particular subject area. From a teaching point of view the issue is how to approach a subject in a way that will enhance the learner's capacity to think independently in that subject (for example, providing a framework that orients learners to the literature and methods of the discipline, to its conceptual tools, to the problems and issues posed, and to the state of knowledge in the discipline). Also, the learner may need to have an understanding of the historical development of the subject and the controversies within it. Fostering the spirit of and capacity for critical inquiry requires a balance of expert input on substantive content, modeling of the critical thought process, and guidance of learners in developing their ability to understand and analyze the subject matter. This version of promoting autonomy, like the humanistic version, can be challenged for failing to address the social and political contexts of learning. This failure is redressed by the critical approach to teaching and learning.

Encouraging critical reflection is of course a long-held value in education, especially in education for social justice, such as in the work of Freire (1972, 1974) with his concept of "conscientization" (see Chapters Four and Seven of this book). Such prominent adult educators as Brookfield (1995, 2005) and (Mezirow, 2000, 2003, 2009) have their own versions of conscientization. For Mezirow it is "transformative learning," which is "learning that transforms problematic frames of reference—sets of fixed assumptions and expectations (habits of mind, meaning perspectives, mindsets)—to make them more inclusive, discriminating, open, reflective, and emotionally able to change. Such frames of reference are better than others because they are more likely to generate beliefs and opinions that will prove more true or justified to guide action" (Mezirow, 2003, pp. 58–59). Mezirow takes up a central concept in adult education—the idea of the autonomous learner—but it is autonomy forged not in the humanistic tradition but in the critical social theory tradition. This gives it a new complexion: it includes the idea of critical awareness. A mature, autonomous learner is critically aware of his or her needs and is able to make a commitment to learning on the basis of a knowledge of genuine alternatives.

Brookfield (1995, 2005, 2008) has developed critical reflection and critical thinking as the centerpiece of this approach to adult education. In his analysis of Nelson Mandela's autobiography *Long Walk to Freedom* he is very explicit about the political nature of critical reflection:

> In using critical reflection as the conceptual hermeneutic through which Mandela's book can be analyzed, I am building specifically on my own politicized formulation of critical reflection as the deliberate uncovering and challenging of assumptions concerning power and the perpetuation of hegemony. Critical reflection is not just thinking deeply about assumptions; rather, it has a specific political purpose. What makes reflection *critical* is its grounding in the critical theory tradition, a tradition that uses reflection to theorize and strategize how to bring about democratic socialism

(Brookfield, 2005). Here, reflection's focus is on under-standing the dynamics of power (and how to manipulate these) and on uncovering (and combating) ruling class hegemony [Brookfield, 2008, p. 96].

Although Brookfield has politicized the idea of critical reflection, his common ground with Mezirow remains. They both emphasize the constraints on learning that originate in the social structure and that become internalized by the learner. Thus they don't accept at face value the beliefs and values of learners—quite the contrary, the whole point of education is, they believe, to challenge accepted beliefs and values. This is what separates theirs from the humanistic point of view. In the critical theory approach the teacher is anything but neutral, always challenging learners' assumptions within a framework that recognizes the power of social forces to shape needs, wants, and desires. Autonomy is not assumed; rather it is something that needs a great deal of work to develop and maintain.

Perhaps the best and most recent attempt to capture the vari-ous aspects of autonomy is contained in the final reports of the Organisation for Economic Cooperation and Development's Definition and Selection of Key Competencies Project (known as the DeSeCo Project), which was established to document the key "competencies for personal, social and economic well-being" (OECD, 2003b, p. 5) in the twenty-first century. This project has been closely linked with the Programme for International Student Assessment (PISA), which is now well entrenched as a global initiative that assesses school-age students' knowledge and skills in the areas of reading, mathematics, science, and problem solving. It was always acknowledged within the Directorate for Education of the OECD that success in life is based on a wider range of competencies than those assessed under PISA, and so the DeSeCo Project was initiated with this in mind. The DeSeCo Project, which was managed by Dominique Rychen (see Rychen and Salganik, 2001), identified three key competencies for a "successful life" and a "well functioning society" as the abilities to "interact in socially heterogeneous groups"; to "act autonomously"; and to "use tools interactively." The report expands on the idea of autonomy:

> Acting autonomously does not mean functioning in social isolation. On the contrary, it requires an awareness of one's environment, of social dynamics and of the roles one plays and wants to play. It requires individuals to be empowered to manage their lives in meaningful and responsible ways by exercising control over their living and working conditions. Individuals must act autonomously in order to participate effectively in the development of society and to function well in different spheres of life including the workplace, family life and social life. This is because they need to develop independently an identity and to make choices, rather than just follow the crowd. In doing so, they need to reflect on their values and on their actions [Organisation for Economic Cooperation and Development (OECD), 2003a, p. 14].

An overarching competency is described as follows: "Reflectivity— a critical stance and reflective practice—has been identified as the required competence level to meet the multifaceted demands of modern life in a responsible way . . . an overall development of critical thinking and a reflective integrated practice based on formal and informal knowledge and experience of life" (OECD, 2001, p. 4).

In regard to the OECD's conception of autonomy, the group acknowledges the key aspects of autonomy present in the academic literature: the importance of action, the link between autonomy and relatedness, reflectivity, critical thinking, agency, and choice. Autonomy is thus not possible without the sociocultural context in which it is situated and becomes meaningful.

How proponents of both the humanistic and liberal approaches conceive autonomy seriously limits their capacity to develop strategies for educating across difference. Among learners from diverse backgrounds it would be a grave error of judgment to regard autonomy as a shared attribute or even as a desirable goal. This is because the psychological subject of autonomy is the separate, bounded, rational individual who stands outside of history, society, and culture, rather than the emotional, embodied, and historically and culturally embedded individual. However, it is only the latter conception that allows us to connect to and have some dialogue with learners based on their life experiences as members of, say, particular racial or ethnic groups. In the critical approach, autonomy cannot be addressed without a critique of systemic inequality and the language, practices, and structures supporting such inequality. For example, critical race theory, which derives from critical theory but has racism as its central construct, portrays racism as a normal rather than an aberrant state of affairs in the United States. This realization calls for a set of strategies very different from those evident in liberal democracies, which, for example, attempt to make race "neutral" or "irrelevant" in the interests of equality before the law but fail to restructure institutions and systems (see Closson, 2010). Alfred (2010) supports this view in characterizing the different views of blacks and whites concerning racial inequality and injustice: "Whites look at matters of racial discrimination with detachment, whereas Blacks view racism in terms of their and their relatives' experiences in past and present encounters with White people" (p. 205). No doubt this applies to other areas of discrimination and inequality, such as gender, ableness, ethnicity, sexual orientation, and age. For teachers and policymakers the challenge is to combine critical thinking about systemic inequalities with a willingness to engage with emotion and affect and to be fully present to others' experiences (see Paxton, 2010). If learners adopt such a stance, they too can be said to have developed what may be called a "critical autonomy."

4

The Repressed Self

In this chapter I present some key concepts in psychoanalysis, such as the unconscious, the divided nature of our mental life, and the sacrifices made by the self in order to participate in civilized life. I also provide a treatment of the implications of psychoanalysis and its applications to education. In so doing I am focusing primarily on the paradigmatic approach of Sigmund Freud, while at the same time being mindful of the development of psychoanalysis up to the present.

Although Freud is often treated as a historical curiosity in standard undergraduate psychological texts, there is no denying his immense and continuing impact on psychology, sociology, anthropology, literature, education, and the arts. During his lifetime Freud was a prolific writer, detailing clinical case studies and developing the practice and theory of psychoanalysis. It is not possible, in a short chapter, to do justice to the intricacies and subtleties of Freud's work and its subsequent developments, especially considering that *The Standard Edition of the Complete Psychological Works of Sigmund Freud* (edited by Strachey, 1953–1974) alone runs into twenty-four volumes. Any condensed treatment is bound to be incomplete and selective. However, for me, the importance of Freud and psychoanalysis more broadly lies in that it allowed us to imagine human beings in a completely different way. Three key features of this new imagining were

1. That we have an *unconscious* dimension to our mental life—repressed thoughts and feelings—making it possible that we can have motives for our behavior of which we are unaware

2. That we have a mental life that is neither coherent nor autonomous—instead there are inner divisions in our mental functioning

3. That social values are internalized as a constituent part of our (divided) "self"

Each of these features has a long history of elaboration, refinement, application, and contestation within subsequent psychoanalytic theories and beyond. In what follows I will attempt to exemplify each of these features with the aim of providing the reader with some insight into the psychoanalytic sensibility.

The Unconscious

In a Freudian psychoanalytic sense there is a fundamental conflict in the human condition: on the one hand, we are dependent on ordered social life to meet our needs; on the other hand, ordered social life necessarily constrains our basic instinctual needs, which are essentially antisocial. In this way our instinctual needs are repressed, and the external conflict between the self and society becomes internalized as psychological conflict. Because repression is a necessary part of the human condition, we can never truly be ourselves. However, we can be more or less repressed, with different consequences for our psychological health and happiness.

Central to the concept of repression is a distinction between what is conscious and what is unconscious in our psychological makeup. Memories, thoughts, and feelings are said to be repressed when they are no longer part of our conscious awareness. In his early work as a physician in late-nineteenth-century Vienna, Freud observed the use of hypnosis as a means of treating a variety of psychological conditions. Two hypnotic phenomena were particularly important for Freud's conceptualization of the unconscious. The first is the phenomenon of posthypnotic suggestion, whereby people have actions suggested to them during hypnosis that they then carry out once they are brought out of hypnosis. The second phenomenon is the apparent ability of people to recapture, under hypnosis, otherwise forgotten memories. He writes about posthypnotic suggestion:

> The well-known experiment . . . of the "post-hypnotic suggestion" teaches us to insist upon the importance of the distinction between *conscious* and *unconscious*. . . . [In this experiment] a person is put into a hypnotic state and is subsequently aroused. While he was in the hypnotic state, under the influence of the physician, he was ordered to execute a certain action at a certain fixed moment after his awakening, say half an hour later. He awakes, and seems fully conscious and in his ordinary condition; he has no recollection of his hypnotic state, and yet at the pre-arranged moment there rushes into his mind the impulse to do such and such a thing, and he does it consciously, though not knowing why [Freud, 1958, p. 261].

The phenomenon of posthypnotic suggestion demonstrates that we are not always aware of our motives for our actions. The corollary of this is the observation that people under hypnosis are able to recall previously forgotten events, thus strengthening the evidence that not all mental life is accessible to conscious awareness. Much of the theory and practice of psychoanalysis rests upon this fundamental insight. But what is the nature of the relationship between the conscious and the unconscious? This was a crucial question for Freud, and once again we find him looking to hypnosis for the answer. Freud noted Bernheim's efforts to promote the recall of hypnotic experiences, such recall demonstrating, at least in principle, that the unconscious was accessible to the conscious person. Freud subsequently set out to identify the importance of the unconscious in psychic life, how to gain access to it, and the processes by which it operated:

> Psychoanalysis sets out to explain . . . uncanny disorders; it engages in careful and laborious investigations . . . until at length it can speak thus to the ego: "A part of the activity of your own mind has been withdrawn from your knowledge and from the command of your will . . . you are using one part of your force to fight the other part. . . . A great deal more must be going on in your mind than can be known to your consciousness. Come, let yourself be taught . . . ! What is in your mind does not coincide with what you are conscious of; whether something is going on in your mind and whether you hear of it, are two different things. In the ordinary way, I will admit, the intelligence which reaches your consciousness is enough for your needs and you may cherish the illusion that you learn of all the more important things. But in some cases, as in that of an instinctual conflict, your intelligence service breaks down. . . . In every case, the news that reaches your consciousness is incomplete and often not to be relied on. . . . Turn your eyes inward, . . . learn first to know yourself!" It is thus that psychoanalysis has sought to educate the ego [Freud, 1954, pp. 142–143].

Psychoanalysis is thus based on the capacity to identify and interpret connections between the recall, associations, feelings, and symptoms of the patient. An underlying tenet is that nothing in mental life occurs randomly and that meaning can be found in the apparently trivial (such as placing a cap on a chair, which requires removal for a person to sit down); the quirky (including various types of compulsive behavior, such as counting all the cracks in the pavement before you can proceed along the path); and the commonplace (such as placing a hot drink in the freezer). The practice of psychoanalysis is based on this proposition: "He that has eyes to see and ears to hear may convince himself that no mortal can keep a secret. If his lips are silent, he chatters with his fingertips; betrayal oozes out of him at every pore. And thus the task of making conscious the most hidden recesses of the mind is one which is quite possible to accomplish" (Freud, 1953, pp. 77–78).

Thus in Freud's clinic, patients were encouraged to report whatever came to their mind, no matter how trivial or embarrassing. His clinical exploration of the unconscious in this way enabled Freud to outline, among others things, the structure of personality.

The Divided Self

Freud's concept of the unconscious is inextricably linked to his description of the basic structures of personality. He distinguishes between three components of personality: the id, ego, and superego. The id is a reservoir of instinctual energy present at birth. It operates by discharging instinctual energy without regard to reality. Nevertheless it is guided by two principles: the Nirvana Principle, which seeks to reduce the excitation of the organism, and the Pleasure Principle, which seeks to increase pleasure and decrease pain. The only mechanism it has at its disposal to attain these goals is to wish for them. Although wishing functions to reduce tension in the short term, ultimately the organism must take reality into account if its wishes are to be fulfilled. Thus for Freud there is no such thing as a preexisting self—all we have are primitive drives, but these are insufficient for living in a world with others, and we need to take into account the reality of these others and the demands they make on us.

This need to perceive reality leads to the development of the ego. Although the ego continues to pursue pleasure and avoid pain, it also operates according to the Reality Principle:

it perceives, remembers, thinks, and acts on the world. It thus performs a mediating role between the instinctual wishes of the id and the actions that will satisfy it. Given that the ego adapts to reality and that part of this reality is social, the ego must therefore *understand* the moral and ethical codes of society, its values, ideals, and taboos. This understanding is necessary for the ego to assess the likely consequences of a given course of action. For example, it might understand that violating a moral code in the pursuit of pleasure will result in some form of punishment by an external agent, perhaps the parent. A crucial insight of Freud's is that during the course of development, sanctions for wrongdoing become internalized and self-administered via one's conscience. In this way the third component of personality structure, the superego, emerges.

> Even if conscience is something "within us" yet it is not so from the first. In this it is a real contrast to sexual life, which is in fact there from the beginning of life and not only a later addition. But, as is well known, young children are amoral and possess no internal inhibitions against their impulses striving for pleasure. The part which is later taken on by the super-ego is played to begin with by an external power, by parental authority. . . . It is only subsequently that the secondary situation develops where the external restraint is internalized and the super-ego takes the place of the parental agency and observes, directs and threatens the ego in exactly the same way as earlier the parents did with the child [Freud, 1973, p. 93].

The superego represents the internalized claims of morality, which enables us to make judgments concerning the worthiness of our actions. When thoughts or actions violate social prescriptions, they are censured by the conscience, and feelings of guilt or shame are generated. In contrast, thoughts or actions that fit with our idealized abstraction of parental or social values (our ego ideal) give rise to feelings of pride and self-esteem. It is important to note here that the ego, in its executive function, is most similar to what others regard as the "self"—but the ego does not have autonomy because it needs to negotiate the demands of the id, superego, and external reality (see Vanheule and Verhaeghe, 2009). Thus there is no such thing as an a priori self—the ego is constructed through interacting with others. Our sense of self comes into being in relation to others and develops over time. Freud describes individual development in terms of a series of stages, called "psychosexual stages": the oral, anal, phallic (with its celebrated Oedipus complex), and genital. The stages basically describe the development of the ego and its growing capacity to control and mediate the unconscious impulses and demands of the id and superego.

Although the unconscious can never be fully harmonized with the conscious, the general notion of understanding aspects of the unconscious and bringing them to the surface was a goal of psychoanalytic psychotherapy. This goal was strengthened in some of the subsequent developments in psychoanalysis, especially in the "ego psychology" in the United States, which stressed the strengthening of the ego's role as "captain of the soul" (see Parker, 2008, pp. 151–152). A strong ego is able, within limits, to deal with the anxiety-producing demands of the id and the superego, but when the ego is overwhelmed a variety of psychological symptoms invariably appears as the ego attempts to "defend" itself. Hence the origin of the term *defense mechanisms*, which include denial (denying reality), projection (attributing one's negative feelings onto others), regression (reverting to childlike behaviors), and reaction formation (acting in a way opposite to actual feelings). The behaviors associated with defense mechanisms can appear within the range of normal functioning (for example, blaming others for a personal failure), or they can appear as quite abnormal (for example, continuing to set the table for a spouse who has died). (See Anna Freud, *The Ego and the Mechanisms of Defense*, 1946, for an original and full treatment.)

Self and Society

Freud's view of the structure of personality implies that there is a necessary conflict between self and society. The person is caught in a dilemma: the basic instincts, which derive from bodily needs, are essentially antisocial, but the cooperation of others is necessary for instinctual gratification. However, the cooperation of others is only made possible through submitting to ordered social life, which of course demands a degree of instinctual renunciation (for example, the restriction of aggressiveness). Freud explores the ramifications of this dilemma in *Civilization and Its Discontents*, in which he argues that the external conflict between individual needs and ordered social life is reflected in an internal psychological conflict among the structures within one's personality:

> What means does civilization employ in order to inhibit the aggressiveness which opposes it, to make it harmless, to get rid of it, perhaps? . . . What happens in him [that is, people in general] to render his desire for aggression innocuous? Something very remarkable, which we should never have guessed and which is nevertheless quite obvious. His aggressiveness is interjected, internalized; it is, in point of fact, sent back to where it came from—that is, it is directed towards his own ego. There it is taken over by a portion of the ego, which sets itself over against the rest of the ego as super-ego, and which now, in the form of "conscience," is ready to put into action against the ego the same harsh aggressiveness that the ego would have liked to satisfy upon

other, extraneous individuals. The tension between the harsh super-ego and the ego that is subjected to it, is called by us the sense of guilt; it expresses itself as a need for punishment. Civilization, therefore, obtains mastery over the individual's dangerous desire for aggression by weakening and disarming it and by setting up an agency within him to watch over it, like a garrison in a con-quered city [Freud, 1963, pp. 60–61].

This helps make sense of Freud's somewhat cryptic remark that the price we pay for civilization is a heightened sense of guilt—the values and norms of ordered social life (that is, civilization) are internalized so that when we transgress, guilt follows. It also places in perspective Fromm's take on Freud's rather pessimis-tic portrayal of the human condition: "Progress, beyond a certain point . . . is in principle impossible. Man is only a battlefield on which the life and death instincts fight each other. He can never liberate himself decisively from the tragic alternative of destroy-ing others or himself" (Fromm, 1973, p. 66).

Freud, so it seems, set an upper limit on our capacity for happi-ness and psychological health, largely because the self is necessar-ily divided.

Psychoanalysis and Education

It is worth pointing out that Freud anticipated the potential of psychoanalysis to inform education: "There is one topic which I cannot pass over so easily—not, however, because I understand particularly much about it or have contributed very much to it. Quite the contrary: I have scarcely concerned myself with it at all. I must mention it because it is so exceedingly important, so rich in hopes for the future, perhaps the most important of all the activities of analysis. What I am thinking of is the application of psychoanalysis to education" (Freud, 1964, p. 146).

This is a surprising statement, so it is worth speculating about this further, in a sense, on behalf of Freud. Perhaps the first and most important point is that education is a form of socialization into a culture. Given Freud's position that culture must necessarily suppress instinctual energies, then so too must education necessary suppress those it educates. Freud was actually quite explicit on this:

> The child must learn to control his instincts. It is impossible to give him liberty to carry out all his impulses without restriction. . . . Accordingly, education must inhibit, forbid and suppress and this is abundantly seen in all periods of history. But we have learnt from analysis that precisely this suppression of instincts involves the risk of neurotic illness. . . . Thus education has to find its way between the Scylla of non-interference and the Charybdis of frustration. . . . An optimum must be discovered which will enable education to achieve the most and damage the least. . . . A moment's reflection tells us that hitherto education has fulfilled its task very badly and has done children great damage [Freud, 1964, p. 149].

At the outset, then, education has an impossible task of balancing the needs of learners with the need for society to produce citizens who can take their place in ordered social life. Historically education has had a bad name in this regard, stressing the authority of the institution, the authority of the discipline, and the authority of the teacher. Since the time of Freud there has no doubt been a progressive liberalization of education, and educational theory and practice have moved toward being learner centered. It would be drawing a long bow to claim that this was in response to psychoanalysis, but psychoanalysis certainly contributed to this trend throughout the twentieth century and into the twenty-first century. Of course there were some schools specifically set up in response to the insights of psychoanalysis, the most notable being Summerhill in the United Kingdom. Such schools attempted to stress the positive and liberating side of education. Others, however, saw psychoanalytic theory as providing a critique of education, so much so that education could be done away with altogether.

Anna Freud (1960) observes this anti-education thrust of psychoanalysis: "Psychoanalysis, whenever it has come into contact with pedagogy, has always expressed the wish to limit education. Psychoanalysis has brought before us the quite definite danger arising from education" (pp. 95–96). Indeed the process of psychoanalysis can be seen as undoing the damage of education. Although education may have a case to answer, the question is whether education, and "culture" more broadly, are necessarily suppressive. The answer for some of those who followed in Freud's footsteps is a resounding no.

A completely different and somewhat more critical approach to the role of society in relation to the self was advocated by such politically radical psychoanalytic thinkers as Reich (1972) and Marcuse (1969), who rejected the idea that instinctual gratification and ordered social life are incompatible. They regard repression (and its associated concepts, such as the Oedipus complex) not as a necessary product of the human condition but as the product of a specific type of social organization, namely, the patriarchal authoritarian one. For example, Reich claims that such antisocial impulses as aggression are secondary, resulting from the repression of natural biological needs. He thus rejects the notion of antisocial instincts. "Moral regulation represses and keeps from gratification the natural biological needs. This results in secondary pathological anti-social impulses. These in turn have to be inhibited of necessity. Thus, morality does not owe its existence to the necessity of inhibiting anti-social tendencies" (Reich, 1972, p. 22).

Marcuse (1969), in *Eros and Civilisation*, argues that Freud failed to distinguish between the level of repression required to maintain "civilized" society as such and the level that would result in an oppressive social structure. Both Reich and Marcuse recognized the critical force of psychoanalysis and tapped into its potential as a basis for a theory of oppression—as did others much later (for example, the women's movement and Marxist intellectuals). Indeed psychoanalysis gives us a glimpse of the ways in which the social structure is united to constraints that operate in our personality, principally through the idea that we internalize the social values of our parents and other authority figures, such as teachers. It helps explain how we can come to act against our own best interests and how political, racial, class-based, and sexual oppression can become a constituent part of our personality structure and the conflicts within it. Although theorists such as Reich and Marcuse bemoan the oppressive nature of moral regulation and authoritarian governments, they at least see the potential for harmony between authority and the psychological health of individuals, and this implies a program of reform—in education and in social regulation more broadly.

In this regard the link between social oppression and psychological repression has occupied the attention of educators working with oppressed groups (for example, Freire, 1972; Thompson, 1983; Brookfield, 2005). Psychoanalysis offers us a theory that explains why some members of oppressed groups fail to recognize their oppression and may angrily denounce those who attempt to convince them otherwise. Most notably, Freire's work (1972, 1974) is replete with psychoanalytic sensibilities: he explicitly links authoritarianism in the family to the oppression and domination that characterize certain forms of education. Authoritarian teachers, like authoritarian parents, practice domination and control. He outlines the oppressive workings of what he calls "banking education," of which there are four key features. First, the methods used force students into passive roles within the active-passive dichotomy (for example, "The teacher teaches and the students are taught," "The teacher knows everything and the students know nothing," "The teacher thinks and the students are thought about," and "The teacher disciplines and the students are disciplined" (Freire, 1972, pp. 46–47). Second, the learner, as a kind of container to be filled, is epistemologically passive and therefore stripped of the human agency necessary to be fully human. Third, banking education serves to dominate through a teacher-centered curriculum whereby the learners are not engaged with knowledge. Finally, banking education operates ideologically by presenting culture as nature and not to be questioned.

Freire of course conceives of an education that can be liberating—one that is dialogic and problem-posing. But is there a role for authority in such an education, given there is a tradition of setting authority against freedom? Freire's answer is that in "liberating" or "problem-posing" education, "the teacher-of-the-students and the students-of-the-teacher cease to exist and a new term emerges: teacher-student with students-teachers. The teacher is no longer merely the one who teachers, but one who is himself taught in dialogue with the students, who in turn while being taught also teach. They become jointly responsible for a process in which all grow. In this process, arguments based on 'authority' are no longer valid; in order to function, authority must be *on the side of* freedom, not *against* it" (Freire, 1972, p. 53).

Bingham (2002) poses the question of what "authority on the side of freedom" entails. His answer is simple—it is to use authority to break out of the circuitry of domination and submission. And Freire (1974) provides a good example of what this means, at least in the context of working as an educator with oppressed people. Notably he adopts the term *conscientization* to describe the understanding people come to have of how their very consciousness is shaped by social and historical forces that ultimately work against their own interests. Conscientization implies a critical awareness of the self as a subject who can reflect on the world, act on it, and transform it. Freire developed and applied his ideas while working in Brazil in the early 1960s on literacy programs. He was not interested solely in developing literacy skills; he was also interested in what these skills could do for people, for how they saw themselves and their world:

> We wished to design a project in which we would attempt to move from naïveté to a critical attitude at the same time we taught reading. We wanted a literacy program which would be an introduction to the democratization of culture, a program with men as its Subjects rather than as patient recipients. . . . The more accurately men grasp true causality, the more critical their understanding will be. Their understanding will be magical to the degree that they fail to grasp causality. Further, critical consciousness always submits that causality to analysis; what is true today may not be so tomorrow. Naïve consciousness sees causality as a static, established fact, and thus is deceived in its perception [Freire, 1974, pp. 43–44].

Freire's position is that oppressed and subjugated people lack a critical understanding of their reality in the sense that for them the sociocultural world in which they live is something that is fixed, and to which they must adapt. Furthermore, the world is controlled by magical forces that are inexplicable. This objectification of the sociocultural world and its magical origins fits in with the interests of oppressive social and political structures by making all aspects of a person's situation appear "natural" and therefore unalterable. Freire encouraged participants in his literacy group, as a first step toward critical understanding, to appreciate the distinction between the world of nature (which is unalterable) and the world of culture (which is a social construction and thereby alterable). Thus in the context of learning to read and write participants come to appreciate the distinction between nature and culture. This is the basis for problematizing previously taken-for-granted aspects of everyday life that hitherto seemed unalterable: poor levels of education, housing, clothing, diet, and health. These are now reconceptualized as problems that can be transformed by democratization. And so for Freire, being more conscious and aware of one's world through a critical questioning of taken-for-granted assumptions is a key to democratization, psychologically healthy selves, and the good of society. A less oppressive society is likely to produce less repressed selves.

At this juncture it is clear that psychoanalytic concepts can be used to provide a powerful critique of education. Education, as a cultural product, can be analyzed as a force of oppression and as a vehicle for embedding dominant ideologies within the psychic structures of learners. However, education of the kind advocated by Freire, in which the relationship between teachers and learners allows them to jointly explore knowledge and develop a critical understanding of their world and their place within it, can be liberating.

Looking beyond the preceding discussion, there are many other ways in which psychoanalysis can be seen as having an impact on education. For example, it can be a source of clinical insight into the relationships among learners and between teachers and learners. Anyone with experience teaching small groups (of, say, between ten and thirty people) will testify to the emotional intensity of teaching and learning. This emotional intensity may be partly in response to the way in which teachers are typically positioned as authority figures and as such invoke parental images and associated infantile reactions (for example, the inevitable disappointment when the hopes or fantasies entertained about a teacher are not fulfilled, resulting in hostility or attempts to undermine the teacher). Freud himself gives an account of the emotional dynamic of the pedagogical relationship in his reflections on his old schoolmasters: "These men [speaking of teachers] became our substitute fathers. . . . We transferred on to them the respect and expectations attaching to the omniscient father of our childhood, and we then began to treat them as we treated our own fathers at home. We confronted them with the ambivalence that we had acquired in our own families and with its help we struggled with them as we had been in the habit of struggling with our fathers" (Freud, 1955, pp. 244).

The emphasis on the significance of family dynamics in Freud's writing has been taken up by later psychoanalytic thinkers. For example, the depth psychology of Melanie Klein (1998) focuses our attention on how anxiety is produced, and remains with us in adulthood, as a result of our complete dependency in the early years of life. West et al. (2007) argue that "relatively little attention has been paid to such tensions in adult and lifewide learning and the way in which the past can invade and paralyse the present" (p. 236). For example, teachers too may feel anxiety about not addressing all the needs of the students and bring to the classroom a set of expectations, fears, and aspirations, some of which may be based on childhood conflicts they have failed to work through. Teachers typically fear criticism, hostility, and losing control—and where fear is present an infantile response from the teacher may follow (varying from becoming overly apologetic and self-effacing about a small mishandling of an event or not being able to criticize students' work to attacking students or refusing to admit an error). Salzberger-Wittenberg, Henry, and Osborne (1983) capture this dynamic quite nicely, arguing that teachers need to be aware of their own infantile desires and resist the temptation to give in to the students' demand that all their desires be fulfilled:

> The teacher may, for instance, agree that students need "spoon-feeding" and thus be inclined to do most of the work for them. He may not realise that, in acceding to their infantile wishes, he is not only pampering them

and undermining their innate capacities, but at the same time satisfying his own wish that learning should be easy. Equally, a teacher who has been, or longed to be, his parents' special child may gain vicarious satisfaction when he bestows special attention on his favorite pupil. (The rest of the class will have to suffer the pangs of jealousy which the teacher has never been able to cope with adequately.) These modes of behaviour encourage dependency and hamper students from coming to grips with reality . . .

The inclination to indulge students may receive further reinforcement from the teacher's fear that any frustration will lead to an outburst of unlimited anger. If the teacher himself is inclined to react with violent rage to the absence of gratification, it will make him so frightened of his students' hostile attacks that he may be unable to enforce limits [Salzberger-Wittenberg et al., p. 50].

It is important not to attribute such negative psychological dynamics solely to the kind of banking education so criticized by Freire. Psychological dynamics of the kind just illustrated are likely to be present in both banking and problem-posing education; however, the response in each case will be quite different. Whereas in banking education the recourse will be to the authority of the teacher, in problem-posing, dialogic education the recourse will be to an open, critical exploration of the issues. However, such a commitment by the teacher does not guarantee that the psychological dynamics will be resolved—this is too much to expect of an experienced analyst, let alone an educator.

Psychoanalysis can also have an impact on education in that the process of psychoanalysis is itself a pedagogical experience, leading to new knowledge not previously available to conscious awareness. Felman (1982) comments: "Psychoanalysis institutes, in this way, a unique and radically original mode of learning. . . . Proceeding not through linear progression, but through break-throughs, leaps, discontinuities, regressions, and deferred action, the analytic learning-process puts in question the traditional pedagogical belief in intellectual perfectibility, the progressiv-ist view of learning as a simple one-way road from ignorance to knowledge" (p. 27). She goes on to note that ignorance takes on a new dimension in psychoanalytic education: it is not a lack of information or an absence of understanding, but an active process of negation—a refusal to admit to consciousness knowledge that is, in principle, available to conscious awareness. Indeed we have a passion for ignorance and a desire to ignore. In this sense we can learn from ignorance if we seek, as teachers, to explore the resis-tance to knowledge. In psychoanalysis, in order for the analyst to become the patient's teacher, he or she must first be a "student of the patient's knowledge" (Felman, p. 33). In a similar way, in the kind of pedagogy proffered by Freire, the teacher must become a student of the learner's knowledge in order to be effective.

5

The Socially Constructed Self

The line of thought leading to the socially constructed self can be traced back to Plato's *Protagoras* from 380 BCE. This is a creation story told by the eponymous Protagoras in which he describes how Zeus charges Prometheus the Titan with the task of creation, and Prometheus in turn passes it on to Epimetheus. The challenge for Epimetheus was to provide all living things with the requisite capabilities and characteristics for survival in such a way that there is a balance among them.

> There were some to whom he gave strength without swiftness, while he equipped the weaker with swiftness; some he armed, and others he left unarmed; and devised for the latter some other means of preservation, making some large, and having their size as a protection, and others small, whose nature was to fly in the air or burrow in the ground; this was to be their way of escape. Thus did he compensate them with the view of preventing any race from becoming extinct. And when he had provided against their destruction by one another, he contrived also a means of protecting them against the seasons of heaven; clothing them with close hair and thick skins sufficient to defend them against the winter cold and able to resist the summer heat, so that they might have a natural bed of their own when they wanted to rest; also he furnished them with hoofs and hair and hard and callous skins under their feet. . . . Thus did Epimetheus, who, not being very wise, forgot

that he had distributed among the brute animals all the qualities which he had to give—and when he came to man, who was still unprovided, he was terribly perplexed [Plato, n.d.].

So at the point at which he thought his work complete, Epimetheus looked around and saw an obvious oversight: humans had been left naked and without any qualities! Plato's principal interest in *Protagoras* was in identifying which of our capacities are learned and therefore the proper subject of education. But as Winkler (2007), citing Heidegger, points out, the story has broader import. Given that we were left to our own devices, we were thus forced by necessity to improvise and shape our environment to overcome our lack of natural protection. We became the great inventors, which necessitated the development of "interior" psychological qualities, such as curiosity, creativity, imagination, experimentation, and a capacity to infer relationships between disparate observations. Perhaps most significant, we became driven by a sense of incompleteness, that there is always something more to be discovered or invented both in the external world and in ourselves. Without any qualities created for us, we effectively became the authors of our own nature, our history, and our biography.

Self and Others

My first encounter with a contemporary exposition of a similar line of argument was with the work of Berger and Luckmann (1967) in their seminal publication, *The Social Construction of Reality*. They added the proposition that much of our nature, history, and biography is in fact socially constructed. My interest at the time paralleled psychology's long-standing interest in reconciling social explanations with existing psychological explanations of the self and psychological phenomena, such as cognition.

In mid-twentieth-century psychology the extreme formulations of behaviorism, as exemplified in the work of Skinner (1973), seemed unsatisfactory as a way of explaining the influence of the external world on the development of the person. For Skinner, organisms (that is, humans) simply emit responses, which are gradually shaped by their consequences. In this framework the self is reduced to a "repertoire of behaviour appropriate to a given set of contingencies. . . . The picture which emerges from a scientific analysis is not of a body with a person inside, but of a body which is a person in the sense that it displays a complex repertoire of behaviour" (pp. 194–195).

"Social being" is thus reduced to "social behavior," just as the very concept of the person is reduced to behavior only. At the time, social learning theorists, such as Bandura (1969), acknowledged the need to include internal cognitive variables in a theory of learning, pointing to the phenomenon of observational learning. Observational learning—that is, learning from the consequences of others' behavior—requires the observer to abstract common attributes from different observations. Thus the learner is actively involved in the construction of a "rule" (or structure, if you like) governing a number of observations. This is important because it means that "social being" is more than simply "social behavior" in that it also incorporates the notion of "social knowledge." The person's knowledge that other people (or *organisms*, to use Skinner's term) control and disburse rewards and punishments enters into the explanation of social development. Such knowledge is not possible without the capacity to distinguish between self, others, and objects. Thus an incipient idea in social learning theory (which was never explored within that tradition) is that the interaction of self and others is a central process in the formation of the person.

This idea of the interaction of self and others was the foundation of both Mead's and Berger and Luckmann's approach to the developing self. A central idea in Mead (1934/1972) is the differentiation of self and other in the development of the individual. For Mead, the development of that uniquely human ability, the ability to communicate through language, is predicated on the ability to take the attitude or role of the other and construe the self as the object of another's experience. The self is essentially socially constructed in that it receives its stability and continuity from taking the role of the "generalized other," which is the attitude of the whole community: "Getting these broad activities of any given social whole or organised society within the experiential field of any one of the individuals involved or included in that whole is, in other words, the essential basis and prerequisite of the fullest development of that individual's self—only insofar as he takes the attitudes of the organised social group to which he belongs, towards the organised, co-operative social activity or set of such activities in which that group as such is engaged, does he develop a complete self" (Mead, 1934/1972, p. 219).

For Mead, it is not roles that are internalized, it is the attitude of the generalized other. Berger and Luckmann's approach (1967) is similar; according to them the child discovers the social world through the medium of significant others. It is in face-to-face encounters that the child's experience of herself is built up in the experiences of others. Eventually the child generalizes from the roles and attitudes of specific others to the roles and attitudes of society as a whole: "The formation within consciousness of the generalised other marks a decisive phase in socialization. It implies the internalization of society as such and of the objective reality established therein, and, at the same time, the subjective establishment of a coherent and continuous identity. Society, identity and reality are subjectively crystallized in the same process of internalization" (p.153).

For Berger and Luckmann (1967), the overriding idea is that we are "predestined to construct and inhabit a world with others" (p. 204). They argue that the socially constructed reality that we experience becomes reified for us as an objective reality—as

if it were "natural." This is the result of the process of "legitimation," whereby social reality as a whole "makes sense" and is "self-
evident" and wherein the course of an individual's life is subjectively endowed with meaning within this social reality. Language
itself is a form of legitimation; so too are informal everyday expres-
sions, maxims, and stories that circulate in the culture. Explicit
theories relating to the conduct of human affairs and the symbolic
universe that we inhabit constitute further levels and types of legitimation, all of which contribute to the acceptance of society and its
activities and prescriptions for conduct as objectively real and subjectively meaningful. For Berger and Luckmann, humans, unlike
animals, are "world-open"—that is, they are open to being socialized in many different ways, largely because their development proceeds over a long period of interaction with the external world.

The Social Organization of the Life Span

Casual observation of how the lifecourse is framed by institutional
practices and values seems to support the arguments of Berger and
Luckmann (1967) in that it is abundantly clear that age-related
norms, statuses, and roles are features of social organization. In
different cultures and historical periods there are different conceptions of the stages of life—their boundaries, dimensions, and
divisions. There are different conceptions of what it means to be a
fully developed person, the processes through which development
occurs, and the significant tasks and marker events in life.

A central feature of modern Western society is a conception of the lifecourse with its distinct phases or stages of infancy,
childhood, adolescence, adulthood, and old age. Arguably much
of social life is organized around socially standardized age categories. In this sense we live in an age-graded society. This institutionalization of the life is necessarily accompanied by external
constraints on individual action (for example, sanctions for not
behaving in an age-appropriate way) or, more important, a set

of expectations about the proper progression of events and roles throughout our lives. Ultimately this influences how we experience ourselves and our relationships with others. For example, we typically develop a posture and attitude toward ourselves as belonging to an age category. That is, we take on the psychological characteristics deemed to be appropriate for our age category (for example, in old age it may be fragility, dependence, forgetfulness) in order to help govern our relationships with those in other age categories. If we fail to act in an age-appropriate manner, we will be seen as deviant by others, who will react at best with mild amusement, perplexity, or perhaps a few patronizing comments, and at worst with anger, fear, or moral outrage.

Some features of and propositions about age structuring and how it relates to the lifecourse of individuals are worth noting. First, age structuring is a universal phenomenon, although it takes particular forms in different cultures and historical periods. Second, age structures, like other social structures, such as gender and class, become a constituent part of our psychology. This means that an understanding of the lifecourse requires an understanding of how individuals engage and struggle with socially prescribed age categories. Third, socially constructed age categories are continuously changing and remain contestable, as do the patterns of individual lives. Individual and social change are related, but they are not necessarily synchronized, which means there can be disjunctions between individual and social change (leading to some individuals' being "out of step" with their generational contemporaries).

The most obvious forms of the institutionalization of the lifecourse are state intervention and regulation—ubiquitous in Western societies—that are aimed at maintaining common life trajectories. The state typically legislates, standardizes, and provides financial and infrastructure support for entry into and exit from formal education, employment, professional practice, marriage, and even life itself (through birth and death certificates).

There are a range of regulatory bodies and mechanisms that distribute resources and opportunities to ensure an orderly progression through the various age categories and divisions within them. These are targeted toward such areas as child support; the commencement, progression, and termination of schooling; the transition from secondary schooling to postsecondary education (with scholarships, apprenticeships, and job search schemes only available to a particular age category); retirement, in which superannuation and other retirement schemes are available; and late adulthood, with government pension schemes and eldercare facilities. Nongovernmental organizations also spread opportunities and resources to enhance an individual's progression through a socially approved, age-based timetable of "successful" career, family, or personal development. This institutionalization of the lifecourse, and the co-option of society at large, make it difficult for individuals to chart alternative lifecourses, at least without considerable financial or personal cost.

There are of course a number of forces moving against the continued institutionalization of the lifecourse that have opened up opportunities for people to be "out of step" with expected trajectories, such as access to higher education for older adults, access to fertilization technologies for older mothers, and a general spirit that challenges prevailing expectations about how we should act at different ages. This spirit of challenging prevailing expectations has also been driven by the growing recognition of different cultural perspectives in academic and everyday life. Different cultures and subcultures clearly have different normative life patterns and may have very different conceptions of what constitutes a fully developed person. Merriam and Kim (2008), for example, explore the nature of indigenous knowledge systems and indigenous views of learning and development. They highlight three aspects of indigenous knowledge systems. First, learning and the construction of identity are regarded as communal: "The individual . . . does not learn for his or her own development, but for what can be contributed to the whole. In some cultures, our Western notion of personal independence and empowerment is considered immature, self-centered, and detrimental to the group" (p. 74). Second, learning and development are holistic and connected to past, present, and future lives; they are embodied, emotional, and spiritual. And finally, learning and development are lifelong and informal, built into everyday life and extending across the life span—they are not seen as distinct activities separated out from other activities. Although it is true that experiential, holistic, and lifelong learning have now entered the educational vernacular in Western countries, these values are driven more by the need to adapt to demands arising from technological, social, and organizational change than by a shared organic culture. But as we shall see in the next section, there is a thread of intellectual enquiry that does indeed focus on the holistic and experiential nature of learning and development.

The Self in Context

A theme in the development of psychology in the late twentieth century has been the growing awareness of the need to take into account the complexities of social context in order to understand the functioning of the mind. This applies as much to intelligence and cognition as it does to theories of the self. Indeed, with the increasing recognition of social context's role in the development of cognition, it becomes impossible to talk of the development of cognition separately from the formation of selves. The processes are the same, as illustrated by tracing the thinking from early constructivist theories of cognition to what has come to be known as the social-constructivist approach to knowledge, or "situated cognition." Generally in the field of cognition there has been a move away from identifying abstract, decontextualized cognitive attributes separated from meaningful action in the world, toward a more inclusive understanding of cognition as it operates through engagement in everyday life. The early work of Piaget set the stage for this development (see Flavell, 1963). His constructivist view of knowledge, particularly in regard to the twin concepts of assimilation (assimilating new experiences into one's existing structures for understanding the world) and accommodation (changing one's structures for understanding the world to fit a new experience), links him to Vygotsky and ultimately to contemporary post-Vygotskian theories of situated cognition.

From a contemporary standpoint it is of course Vygotsky (1978) who is seen as providing a more complete account of the role of historical, social, and cultural forces in development. Daniels (2001) draws attention to Vygotsky's emphasis on the sociocultural nature of human activity and development. A concept central to understanding how culture enters into psychological processes is *mediation*. Vygotsky argues that relations between subjects and objects are mediated by both signs and tools, which function quite differently:

> The tool's function is to serve as the conductor of human influence on the object of activity; it is externally oriented; it must lead to changes in objects. It is a means by which human external activity is aimed at mastering, and triumphing over, nature. The sign, on the other hand, changes nothing in the object of a psychological operation. It is a means of internal activity aimed at mastering oneself; the sign is internally oriented. . . . The mastering of nature and the mastering of behavior are mutually linked, just as man's alteration of nature alters man's own nature. . . . One thing is already certain. Just as the first use of tools refutes the notion that development represents the mere unfolding of the child's organically predetermined system of activity, so the first use of signs demonstrates that there cannot be a single organically predetermined internal system of activity that exists for each psychological function [Vygotsky, p. 55].

He then proceeds to explain how the interpersonal becomes intrapersonal in the child's development: "Every function in the child's development appears twice: first, on the social level, and later, on the individual level; first between people (interpsychological), and then inside the child (intrapsychological). This applies equally to voluntary attention, to logical memory, and to the formation of concepts. All the higher functions originate as actual relations between human individuals. . . . The internalisation of socially rooted and historically developed activities is the distinguishing feature of human psychology" (Vygotsky, 1978, p. 57).

The apparently intractable problem of how the "interpersonal" becomes "intrapersonal," or how the "outside world" comes to be "inside" individual consciousness, has been played out over many years in sociology and psychology. A recent version of this process, one that is important for educators, is provided by Matusov (1998). Following Vygotsky's lead, he distinguishes between internalization and participation models for understanding this process. He presents these models in a true dialectical style, as two different worldviews: the internalization "thesis" and the participation "antithesis" as outlined in Table 5.1.

There are different versions of the internalization and participation models (see Valsiner, 1997; Ratner, 1999), largely separated by their position on the nature or existence of boundaries separating "inner" and "outer" worlds and by the posited level of individual agency and autonomy for the developing human. One's position on these issues clearly has an impact on pedagogical practices, especially when one is considering the nature of the learning activity being undertaken (for example, the role of internal cognitive processes as opposed to collaborative activities) and how learning resources are incorporated into pedagogical practices. Lave and Wenger (1991), to whom we turn in the next section, are firmly located within a "participation" model in their approach to learning in communities of practice.

Table 5. 1 Different Models for Relating the Social to the Psychological

Internalization Thesis	Participation Antithesis
Social and psychological planes are separate, with the social plane preceding the psychological plane in ontogenesis (e.g., development of a child).	Social and psychological planes mutually constitute each other and are inseparable.
Joint and solo activities are separate, with solo activity being psychologically and developmentally more advanced than the corresponding joint activity.	Joint and solo activities mutually constitute each other and are inseparable aspects of sociocultural activity. Sociocultural activities cannot be reduced to mental functions that can, in principal, be performed by one individual.
An individual can take skills and functions from one activity and bring them to another activity.	Skills and functions are embedded in sociocultural activities. The individual exists in the flow of sociocultural activities and cannot transcend them.
The course of development (i.e., its teleology) is objectively defined by human sociocultural nature.	The notion of development, like the notions of activity and learning, is grounded in meaning and thus is distributed, interpreted, and renegotiated.
Development should be studied as a comparison of individual skills and functions before, during, and after a specially designed social intervention aiming to promote "the zone of proximal development" (see Vygotsky, 1978) and internalisation.	Development can be observed and studied as the processes of changes of participation validated by the changing community.

Source: Selected from Matusov, 1998, 326–349.

Learning to Be Through Participation
in Communities of Practice

Lave and Wenger (1991) depart quite radically from traditional ways of conceiving learning and the development of knowledge. For them, learning necessarily arises from participation in a community of practice, which is a community engaged in a common activity with its associated ways of working, stories, and traditions. New members of communities of practice participate in a peripheral way (hence the term *legitimate peripheral participation*), with their participation gradually increasing as they become more engaged and undertake more complex activities. Eventually they become full participants in the sociocultural practices of the community (becoming "old timers": rather than "newcomers"). Lave and Wenger base their views on a variety of studies of rites of passage into communities of practice, such as the informal and family-oriented apprenticeship of Yucatec midwives, the master-apprentice arrangements in the training of butchers, and the recruitment and training of quartermasters. They comment on the ways in which learning is mediated through participation in the activities of those communities, with a focus on how learners in quite divergent communities move from peripheral to full participation. In this regard they point to the importance of having direct access to what is to be learned, and how the physical layout and the culture of work enhance or constrain participation by opening or closing opportunities for collaborative work, observation, mentoring, and guidance. For them, instruction is less of a resource for learning than it is access to practice in relevant settings with strong goals for learning.

They bring quite a different mind-set to their conception of learning: it entails a move away from a focus on individual learning and toward community learning. They see learning as an "integral and inseparable aspect of social practice" (Lave and Wenger, 1991, p. 31). Thus they oppose the individualized psychological tradition that emphasizes learning by doing, reflection on experience, and a decentering from the teacher to the learner. Learning is fostered through coparticipants' engaging in a community of practice rather than through individuals' acquiring mastery over knowledge and processes of reasoning. Learning is thus "situated" in practice, hence the adoption of the term *situated learning*. Allied to this focus on the community of learners is a rejection of the idea that learners acquire cognitive *structures* or *schemata* through which they understand the world. The interest is not in the structure of mental representations of individuals; it is in the structure of participation frameworks.

The main claims of the situated learning project, as exemplified by Lave and Wenger, are twofold: first that it makes no sense to talk of knowledge that is decontextualized, abstract, or general; and second that new knowledge and learning are properly conceived as being located in communities of practice.

Billett (1992, 1996) provides empirical support for Lave and Wenger's thesis in that he shows how different forms of social practice lead to different ways of appropriating and structuring knowledge. He interviewed shift workers in a mining and secondary processing plant to document their learning resulting from both structured learning arrangements at the plant and unstructured daily work practices. He was interested in the value of different learning resources available to workers, such as learning guides, computer-based learning, video presentations, mentors, direct instruction, observing and listening, other workers, everyday activities, and the work environment. His study revealed that the most valued resources were the informal rather than the formal resources. Moreover, these informal resources, described as "everyday activities," "observing and listening," and "other workers," were deemed to be the most valuable for all types of knowledge (propositional knowledge, procedural knowledge, and dispositional knowledge). His study highlights that there are a variety of learning resources in a community of practice (such as other workers, hints, reminders, explanations, observations, the ability to listen, opportunities to deal with authentic problems, one's personal history), and that these influence how knowledge is appropriated and structured.

Much of the literature on situated learning emphasizes the ways in which work practices are central to self-formation. However, Billett (2003) quite rightly warns against an "over-socialized" conception of learning by drawing attention to the unique life histories individuals bring to their participation in social practices:

> Understanding the interdependence between individuals' learning and the social and cultural contributions to that learning is a contested project within psychological thought, as it is within sociology and philosophy. My interest in this interdependence has it origins in the representations of knowledge of hairdressers which yielded a legacy of workplace norms, practices and values that were identified as shaping the conduct of their work. However, contributions beyond the particular workplace were also identified as shaping these individuals' vocational practice thereby also influencing how they worked and learnt through their current work. More than being merely idiosyncratic, these contributions had their genesis in the events in the hairdressers' life histories. So, beyond the immediate social experience, premediate experiences—those occurring earlier—that, in turn, shape their postmediate experiences—those occurring later—need to be accounted for in considering the social geneses of individuals' cognition [Billett, 2003, p. 2].

Thus Billett, unlike Lave and Wenger, adopts a social-cognitive view of the person in that he recognizes that individuals bring unique life experiences to their workplace and that these partly shape their interactions with their workplace community. Andersen, Chen, and Miranda (2002), who also subscribe to a social-cognitive view of the person, provide some insight into how selves interact with communities of practice. Their concept of the entangled self has resonance with the theses of Mead and Berger and Luckmann:

> We subscribe to the assumption that the self is funda-
> mentally relational—that is, entangled with significant
> others—such that key elements of the self are experi-
> enced in relation to significant others, even when others
> are not present. In our social-cognitive model of trans-
> ference, transference occurs when a mental representa-
> tion of a significant other is activated by cues in a new
> person that resemble the other. As a result, the self in
> relation to this significant other is activated, eliciting
> changes in affect, expectancies, motivations, and behav-
> iors, as well as in the nature of the working self-concept,
> all reflecting the version of the self one is when with the
> significant other [Andersen et al., 2002, p. 159].

Within the concept of the entangled self, the self is seen as being inextricably enmeshed in relationships with "significant" others. Significant others are the source of a person's repertoire of selves. Moreover, one's knowledge of oneself is also contextual in the sense that the pool of knowledge about oneself is vast and unlikely to be present in totality in every context—so a particular context, with specific significant others, triggers the person one is in that context. In a sense, "the self is essentially constructed anew in each context. . . . [T]he working self-concept shifts toward the self one is with the significant other" (Andersen et al., 2002, p. 160). We all develop mental representations of significant others, which are a major source of self-definition and self-regulatory processes;

these mental representations resurface (or are transferred) in encounters with new persons and provide a framework for our emotional and behavioral responses to them. This is a social-cognitive view of the person, whereby the condition for developing a self is the capacity to see yourself from the perspective of the other. You come to be and know yourself through the eyes of others. And so participation in a community of practice certainly fosters a new self, but this new self cannot be totally separated from others who are outside the particular community of practice. The self is entangled in more than one community, and no one community of practice is able to socialize you fully in its image.

6

The Storied Self

André Gide's depiction (1902/1960) of his character's struggle to redefine himself invites us to consider life as a narrative construction: "And I compared myself to a palimpsest; I tasted the scholar's joy when he discovers under more recent writing, and on the same paper, a very ancient and infinitely more precious text. What was this occult text? In order to read it, was it not first of all necessary to efface the more recent one?" (p. 51).

The metaphor of the palimpsest suggests the existence of multilayered texts with sediments from the past that have been written over by subsequent texts but that are nevertheless there to be excavated and read anew. In this passage, which was written in the late nineteenth century, Gide prefigures an important later development in the humanities and social sciences—the "turn to narrative" or "discourse" as a way of understanding self-formation.

The idea of narrative is appealing to educators. First, learning, in the sense of meaning-making, can be understood as a narrative process. Second, personal change also can be conceptualized as a narrative process. And finally, the construction of a life narrative can be seen as the central concern of adult development (see Clark and Rossiter, 2008). Often the most immediate concern of teachers is to respond in some way to the stories learners bring to the classroom. These stories are typically located in a particular problem or issue, but they invariably lead to concerns about the self, such as self-esteem, self-satisfaction, well-being, self-doubt, and self-efficacy. One response is to accept the story as true for the person concerned and to work within the boundaries and parameters of the story as it is told. But this places limits

on the teacher: his or her role becomes advisory only, there is
no fundamental challenge to the definition of the problem, and
there is little prospect that the problem will be addressed in all
its complexity. An alternative response is to challenge the story
as it is told with a view to exploring alternative stories about
the self. It is at this point that two quite different approaches to
the narrative become apparent: the reflexive and the relational
(see Chappell et al., 2003). The difference between these two
approaches hinges on their position on two issues. The first issue
is whether it is possible or desirable for self-narration to be targeted toward the construction of a stable, coherent, "bounded"
self as a normative goal (reflexive), or whether such a project is
neither desirable nor possible in a world of multiple and shifting,
open-ended, and ambiguous narratives and identities (relational).
The second is whether a person can construct his or her own self
through a process of self-narration (reflexive), or whether a person is limited by, or is compelled to draw exclusively from, preexisting narratives that are circulating in a particular culture
(relational). The reflexive approach to narrative is neatly captured by Chappell et al.:

> What we have termed here reflexive identification is
> the process through which people come to see them-
> selves as unique individuals who have an identity that
> "belongs" to them. This process allows a person to iden-
> tify with themselves—so, for example, in Western cul-
> ture it is common for us to talk of a "life story" which
> emplots the events of one's life in such a way as to con-
> struct the person as a unique individual whose identity,
> at least in part, endures through that story. Hence, peo-
> ple can talk about their lives, they can write biographies
> and autobiographies that provide a narrative continuity
> of one life that constructs a person as having an identity
> that endures through time [Chappell et al., p. 49].

Self-Narration

The work of McAdams (1996) illustrates the reflexive approach, although it does have relational elements. He views narrative construction as a lens through which the world is seen or as a kind of internal model that is a guide to identity and action. His focus is on the continuity of the self over time and the ways in which we narrate our past, present, and future. For him, identity is the sense of unity, coherence, and purpose in life: it is the experience of a continuous, coherent self—a self that remains essentially the same from one situation to the next and over time, and that is unique, integrated, and different from but related to other selves. In contemporary Western society, the construction of such a self has become problematic, mainly because of the constantly changing and multiple choices we face. It is no longer true that our identity is prescribed or conferred; rather, selves are constructed: "One's very identity becomes a product or project that is fashioned and sculpted, not unlike a work of art. . . . [Moreover,] the developing self seeks a temporal coherence. If the self keeps changing over the long journey of life, then it may be incumbent on the person to find or construct some form of life coherence and continuity to make the change make sense" (McAdams, 1996, p. 297).

McAdams considered identity to be the third of three levels used in gaining an understanding of the person: the other two levels being personality traits (which are broad, comparative dimensions of personality, such as extroversion, dominance, and neuroticism) and "personal concerns," which refer to a variety of psychological constructs, such as motives, values, defense mechanisms, and attachment styles—strategies people use that may differ according to time, place, and context (unlike traits). For example, one's achievement motivation may come into play in sports but not in a professional context, or vice versa. McAdams argued that as one moves from level one to level two, there is a movement toward a more detailed and nuanced understanding of the person over time and in particular situations. What is missing, however, is the concept of identity. An understanding of a person is not complete without understanding his or her overall psychological unity, purpose, and meaning in life.

McAdams holds that our identity is self-constructed (that is, it is constructed reflexively). He thus examines the lifecourse as a narrative or story. For him the lifecourse is "an internalized and evolving narrative of the self that incorporates the reconstructed past, perceived present, and anticipated future" (McAdams, 1996, p. 307). It is both a psychological and a social construction in the sense that it is jointly authored by the person and his or her culture. Life stories render the past, present, and future both meaningful and coherent. Thus the function of a life story is to integrate disparate elements of the self. Based on an analysis of over two hundred accounts of life story interviews, McAdams (1985, 1993) identified the following common features:

- Narrative tone—the emotional tone or attitude (for example, pessimism, optimism, tragedy, romance, irony)

- Imagery—the metaphors and similes that provide the narrative with a distinctive feel

- Theme—the kinds of things that are pursued in the narrative (for example, power, love, recognition, achievement)

- Ideological setting—a moral stance or view of the "good" from which judgments are made of one's life and the lives of others

- Nuclear episodes—scenes and events that stand out in the narrative, normally high points or low points or turning points

- Imagoes—idealized personifications of the self, drawing on archetypal characters and contemporary role models

The features just listed provide a way into an understanding of the life story. But of particular interest is the developmental trajectory of life stories. How do life stories change over time? Here McAdams (1996) distinguished between the following eras:

- The prenarrative era, in which infants, children, and adolescents gather materials for future stories of the self but are not really engaged in the construction of identity proper
- The narrative era, which runs from the beginning of the creation of a self-defining life story (in late adolescence or early adulthood) and continues through most of the adult years
- The postnarrative era, in which life is reviewed and evaluated as a story that is near completion

When one first approaches the construction of a narrative in early adulthood, the typical move is to organize personal values into an ideological system and to select key scenes from the past that explain one's contemporary self and one's anticipated future self (for example, "It was a real turning point when the music teacher said to me, 'You can do it'—it was her confidence in me that got me going, and now I am embarking on a promising music career").

In their twenties and thirties many adults fashion stories around various social roles (imagoes)—for example, caregivers, partners, workers. Midlife brings with it concerns for harmony and reconciliation in the life story and the beginning of the creation of the end of the narrative. Identity formation may turn now to issues of generativity as people begin to define themselves in terms of their legacy. The point being made by McAdams (1996) is that for most of adult life, life stories are continually under construction, and that different themes and concerns emerge at different ages, with periods of intensive and less intensive "identity work" or "selfing." It is important to note that there are multiple stories associated with the diverse ways in which adults live their lives. He nevertheless stipulated the qualities of the "good" story, at least from the perspective of mental health. The elements of such a story are

- Coherence—the extent to which the story makes sense
- Openness—tolerance for change and ambiguity
- Credibility—evidence that the story is grounded in the real world
- Differentiation—the story's complexity
- Reconciliation—harmony and resolution among the multiple components of the self
- Generative integration—a sense that the individual is a productive and contributing member of society

McAdams's approach is similar to the life stage and phase theories of Levinson and Loevinger described in Chapter Three. This is not surprising given that one of the main research tools McAdams used was the biographical interview, and so the raw data for his studies were the stories that people told about themselves across their life span. But McAdams acknowledges the multiple ways in which people find coherence and continuity and meaning in their lives, and he is therefore not attempting to discover the "true" story of the lifecourse as previous studies have attempted to do (see, for example, Levinson, 1978, 1996). For him, experience is a story that can be reinterpreted and reassessed. Moreover, because the self remains situated in history and culture, it is continually open to reinscription and reformulation. But of course we cannot ascribe just any meaning to our experiences, and we cannot create any identity we choose. Our stories must be plausible and credible, and they must contain aspects of the "good" story just outlined.

Narrative Interventions

The implication of McAdams's account for therapeutic or educational intervention is that the purpose should be to explore different ways of viewing the world and different internal models to guide action—to construct a new "replacement" narrative that is more functional and adaptive for the person concerned. The resulting re-authoring of the self has as a normative goal a single, unified, and coherent narrative that resides in the mind of a single individual. Perhaps the best example of this approach in a therapeutic context is provided by Michael White, a key figure in the narrative therapy movement. White (1989, 1991) is a family therapist who directs his energies toward the problems of clients. His basic technique is to externalize these problems; that is, the problems are treated as outside the person. For example, if a child soils his pants regularly, it is usual for family members to see this problem as internal to the child. Talking of the problem as though it were a separate entity involves giving it a name, such as "Sneaky Poo." After naming the problem, White then maps the influence of "Sneaky Poo" on the life of the child and his relationships. Once the problem's sphere of influence has been mapped, he then seeks to map the child's influence in the life of the problem. This leads to the identification of the child's resistance to the problem and his acts of defiance against "Sneaky Poo" that have been written out of the dominant story. These instances of resistance lead to new stories. White (1989) writes of his clients more generally, "I introduced questions that encouraged them to perform meaning in relation to [their] examples, so that they might 're-author' their lives and relationships. How had they managed to be effective against the problem in this way? How did this reflect on them as people and on their relationships? What personal and relationship attributes were they relying on in making these achievements? Did success give them any ideas about further steps that they might take to reclaim their lives from the problem?" (p. 11).

The process of externalizing the problem is seen by White as a counterpractice to oppose cultural practices that objectify persons and their bodies. It enables people to create a distance between themselves and the dominant stories that have been shaping their lives and relationships. It also opens up spaces for people to re-author themselves. Although he manages to avoid individualizing the problem, he still retains the notion of individual responsibility through improving the person's capacity to create new stories and thus develop a heightened sense of personal agency.

White is careful to define the problem to be externalized. For example, in instances of violence and sexual abuse he would be "more inclined to encourage the externalization of the attitudes and beliefs that appear to compel the violence, and those strategies that maintain persons in their subjugation: for example, the enforcement of secrecy and isolation" (White, 1989, p. 12). In such instances his approach would still involve asking the persons involved to tell their story, say, about men's aggression in general and the circumstances leading to particular instances of violence. He would then introduce a new account of the problem, perhaps drawing on patriarchal ideology and how it is supported through various cultural discourses, always with the encouragement to challenge such discourses. In some instances the "problem" is already external to the person, such as when people are attempting to shake off dominant and disqualifying stories that others have about them and their relationships. In such cases White suggests ways in which one's preferred stories can be circulated. The important thing to note about White's therapeutic practice is that he helps individuals gain a sense of personal agency by assisting them in developing counternarratives to oppose detrimental narratives that they have adopted for themselves or that are circulating in the broader culture. He thus has a strong sense that externally existing narratives can be taken up by individuals, to their detriment, and that these narratives therefore can and should be resisted.

The Self as Relational

To return to McAdams (1996), he sees narratives as providing an *internal model* or *internal lens* through which the world is viewed. Gergen and Kaye (1993), who also adopt a narrative approach, see this as rather limiting:

> For many making the postmodern turn in therapy, the narrative continues to be viewed as either a form of internal lens, determining the way in which life is seen, or an internal model for the guidance of action. . . . [T]hese conceptions are found lacking in three important respects. First, each retains the *individualist* cast of modernism, in that the final resting place of the narrative construction is within the mind of the single individual. . . . Secondly, the metaphors of the lens and the internal model both favor *singularity in narrative*, that is, both tend to presume the functionality of a single formulation of self-understanding. The individual possesses a "lens" for comprehending the world, it is said, not a *repository* of lenses; and through therapy one comes to possess "a new narrative truth," it is often put, not a *multiplicity* of truths. . . . Finally, both the lens and the internal model conceptions favor belief in or *commitment to narrative*. That is, both suggest that the individual lives *within* the narrative as a system of understanding. . . . To be committed to a given story of self, to adopt it as "now true for me," is vastly to limit one's possibilities of relating [Gergen and Kaye, p. 254].

For Gergen and Kaye, an alternative is to view the self as relational, whereby a multiplicity of self-accounts are available and new ways of relating to others are explored. Within a therapeutic context, such an approach "encourages the client, on the one hand, to explore a variety of means of understanding the self, but discourages a commitment to any of these accounts as standing for the 'truth of self.' The narrative constructions thus remain fluid, open to the shifting tides of circumstance—to the forms of dance that provide fullest sustenance" (Gergen and Kaye, 1993, p. 255).

The idea of self-narratives' changing according to the relationship in which one is engaged implies a shift from a focus on individual selves coming together to form a relationship to a focus in which the relationship takes center stage, with selves being a by-product of relatedness. The idea of shifting self-narratives to suit the circumstances is one that might seem somewhat self-serving or deceitful, but Gergen and Kaye see this as a misconstrual. They simply wish to emphasize that each portrayal of self operates within the conventions of a particular relationship. As such, adopting different self-narrations for different relationships is "to take seriously the multiple and varied forms of human connectedness that make up life" (Gergen and Kaye, 1993, p. 255). Thus the lifecourse, far from developing in an orderly sequence, is fragmented and discontinuous in a manner poetically captured by Marguerite Yourcenar in her fictional autobiography of the Roman emperor Hadrian:

> The landscape of my days appears to be composed, like mountainous regions, of varied materials heaped up pell-mell. There I see my nature, itself composite, made up of equal parts of instinct and training. Here and there protrude the granite peaks of the inevitable, but all about is rubble from the landslips of chance. I strive to retrace my life to find in it some plan, following a vein of lead, or of gold or the course of some subterranean stream . . . but too many paths lead nowhere at all, and too many sums add up to nothing. To be sure, I perceive in this diversity and disorder the presence of a person; but his form seems nearly always to be shaped

by the pressure of circumstance; his features are blurred,
like a figure reflected in water [Yourcenar, 1959, p. 26].

I should say here that although this fictional autobiography is
set in the time of Hadrian, the writer is adopting a contemporary world sensibility. The question is, How can this very contemporary problem of the stability, continuity, and wholeness of
the person be addressed? This is where I see the relevance of the
biographical narrative, which can be seen as a means of crafting
our own lives in ways that provide a degree of continuity and
coherence. But it can be more than that—it is also a way of coping with change if used reflexively in thinking about how our life
history narratives intersect with our emotional state, our interpersonal relationships, and the social world in which we live.

A somewhat more prosaic way to summarize the work of
Gergen and Kaye (1993) is to say that they attempt to incorporate postmodern theory into contemporary psychology, as evident
in their notion of the relational self, whereby selves are realized
through narratives that surround and define them. But for some
critics, Gergen and Kaye do not go far enough. Rose (1998), after
acknowledging the significance of Gergen's work (see also Gergen
and Gergen, 1988), proceeds to place it firmly within the old psychology camp:

> Such analyses inescapably posit the human agent as
> the core of sense-making activities, in actively nego-
> tiating his or her way through available accounts in
> order to live a meaningful life. Hence the human being
> is understood as that agent which constructs itself as a
> self through giving its life the coherence of a narrative.
> Evidently, "the self," simply by virtue of being capable
> of narrating "himself or herself" in a variety of ways,
> is implicitly reinvoked as an inherently unified out-
> side to these communications. . . . Yet, for our radical

> psychologists it is indeed the familiar old self that is
> invoked, that comforting "I" of humanistic philosophy
> [Rose, p. 177].

This is typical of postmodern critiques of psychology: it is as if psychology, despite its best intentions, just doesn't "get it" and thus can never escape its fate as the "other" of postmodern theory—as a normalizing practice that is a source of regulation and control (see Chapter One). This is because, as the argument goes, psychology sees the problematic of the social within the self as framed in terms of a binary opposition or dualism between the individual and society, as if the two poles "individual" and "society" are antithetical, are separate, and pull in opposite directions. Moreover, it is not possible to escape this dualism by proposing a dialectical interaction between "individual" and "society," because it is inevitable that one needs to explain how the "outside" gets "inside" so to speak. The psychological vernacular is replete with concepts that attempt to do this, such as "internalization," "interaction," "intersubjectivity," "accommodation," "shaping," "role," and "modeling." The reason for their failure, at least from a postmodern point of view, is that they are based on an acceptance of the individual-society dualism. For example, theories that stress shaping and modeling assume a totally passive individual who is molded by external forces. Other theories that employ such concepts as interaction, internalization, accommodation, role, and intersubjectivity, ultimately rely on the existence of a unitary, rational, essential self.

Postmodern Critique of the Psychological Self

A distinguishing feature of postmodernism has been its development of a way of theorizing subjectivity that is not reliant on the individual-society dualism apparent in psychological accounts of the self. It does so by adopting the terms *the subject* and *the social*, which are understood as produced rather than as pregiven and then interacting. For example, the idea of the unitary, coherent, and rational subject as agent, as outlined in Chapter One, is "deconstructed" by postmodern analysis as being a historical product, best understood as a discourse embedded in everyday practices and as part of the productive work of, say, psychology and its associated educational technologies. This view is replaced by the idea of the subject as a position within a discourse. It is important to note that there are a number of discourses, which means a number of subject positions are produced; and because discourses are not necessarily coherent or devoid of contradiction, subjectivity is regarded as multiple, not purely rational, and potentially contradictory. Usher, Bryant, and Johnson (1997) portray the postmodern narrative of the self as "that of a decentred self, subjectivity without a centre or origin, caught in meanings, positioned in the language and narratives of culture. The self cannot know itself independently of the significations in which it is enmeshed. There is no self-present subjectivity, hence no ultimate transcendental meaning of the self. Meanings are always 'in play' and the self, caught up in this play, is an ever-changing self, caught up in the narratives and meanings through which it leads its life" (p. 101). Thus the postmodern self is characterized by "multiple subjectivities," "multiple life-worlds," and "multiple layers."

The postmodern view of the subject has difficulties of its own. The first is that the various theoretical treatments of how a subject comes into being do not altogether escape the notion of an essential, original subject. Hall (1997), for example, argues that Foucault, perhaps the most celebrated postmodernist, comes up against this difficulty, especially in his "archaeological" work (*Madness and Civilization, The Birth of the Clinic, The Order of Things, The Archaeology of Knowledge*), in which, Hall claims, "Discursive subject positions become *a priori* categories which individuals seem to occupy in an unproblematic fashion" (p. 10). Who are these "individuals" who come to "occupy" discursive subject positions? They sound very familiar to the "originary" selves that postmodernism has so strongly criticized. It should be noted here that Foucault's reduction of subjectivity to discourse, and the omission of agency in his conception of subjectivity in his earlier works, was something he came to regret and sought to correct (see Yates and Hiles, 2010).

The second difficulty that postmodern accounts of the subject face concerns the theorization of resistance. Hall (1997), with reference to Foucault's *Discipline and Punish* and *The History of Sexuality*, observes that these works are characterized by "the entirely self-policing conception of the subject which emerges from the disciplinary, confessional and pastoral modalities of power . . . and the absence of any attention to what may in any way interrupt, prevent or disturb the smooth insertion of individuals into the subject positions constructed by these discourses [that Foucault analyzes]" (p. 11).

Thus, at least according to Hall, Foucault sees us as entirely complicit in our own subjugation. This is further illustrated by Usher and Edwards's Foucauldian analysis (1995) of the guidance and counseling of adult learners. They characterize the contemporary period in terms of a shift from disciplinary power (the gaze from the other) to pastoral power (the gaze from within). Evidence of this can be seen in the technologies of self-management in guidance and counseling (for example, learning contracts, self-evaluation, portfolio development) that encourage people to document their lives in every detail and to take responsibility for life planning, self-development, and self-realization. Usher and Edwards argue that in counseling, the self is constituted as an object of knowledge, the task being to discover the "truth" about oneself, which is a form of confessional practice that is ultimately disempowering:

> This process has spread and has now become central
> in the governance of modern society, where externally

imposed discipline has given way to the self-discipline of an autonomous subjectivity. With the spread of confession, its purpose shifts from one of salvation to self-regulation, self-improvement and self-development. In other words, confession actively constitutes a productive and autonomous subject already governed and thereby not requiring externally imposed discipline and regulation. . . . [W]hile confession plays an important role in displacing canonical knowledge by valorising individual experience, this simply extends the range of pastoral power embedded in the confessional regime of truth [Usher and Edwards, pp. 12–13].

Such an analysis is valuable for understanding how we come to discipline ourselves, but for Usher and Edwards, it is not a question of *some* counseling practices producing selves that are disempowering—*all* counseling practices are disempowering in the sense that they are directed toward finding a stable, autonomous identity. This of course challenges those adult education practices that invite self-examination and self-transformation, either collectively or individually, to oppose and resist domination and domestication. These practices have in common a modernist project of developing a self with a semblance of stability, unity, coherence, and continuity, however multiple or subject to change the self might be. In many adult education practices the modern self is seen as a source of resistance to power, rather than as solely an accomplice in its own subjugation. This line of thought can be taken further by turning the postmodern critique on its head: the celebration of the fragmented and unstable postmodern self can be seen as *exactly* what the contemporary labor market needs with its demand for workers who are multiskilled, flexible, and multi-layered. As Kellner (1992) comments, "Wherever one observes phenomena of postmodern culture one can detect the logic of capital behind them" (p. 172).

It is important to note that Foucault conceded late in his life that his earlier work, with its emphasis on "asylums, prisons and so on . . . insisted . . . too much on the question of domination" (Foucault, 1993, p. 204). He thus came to recognize that his work did not deal sufficiently with resistance to power and that he needed to engage in questions of agency, freedom, and creativity—ideas normally associated with coherent selfhood.

Continuity and Coherence in the Self as a Normative Ideal

In opposing the postmodern view, it is possible to argue that some level of continuity and coherence in the self, however fragile, is a necessary condition for resistance to domination and oppression. It is clear that education has a tradition of empowerment based on the modern subject, especially when it is addressing the concerns of those whose sense of self has been dislocated and fragmented through a history of domination and oppression. Supporting this tradition of empowerment, McLaren (1995) observes the irony that "just at a time in history when a great many groups are engaged in 'nationalisms' which involve redefining their status as marginalized Others, the academy [referring here to postmodernism] . . . casts a general skepticism on the possibilities of a general theory which can describe the world and institute a quest for historical progress" (p. 206).

In many educational contexts empowerment is predicated on the pursuit of a coherent, continuous self. Although it is may be true that many of the technologies in counseling and education serve to disempower in the name of individual liberation, the source of disempowerment is located in the production of *particular types* of coherent subjectivities and not in the pursuit of coherence itself. Arguably, in struggles that involve contestations of identity, it is those who have a strong sense of their own self who offer the best potential for resistance. This is not to say that personal change is simply an internal psychological practice conducted in isolation from others; others are always implicated, both immediate others and generalized others (generalized others refers here to institutional and social practices, beliefs, and values). The postmodern sensibility has drawn attention to the role of language as providing the resources for negotiating meaning and, ultimately, "meaningful lives." It is clear that there exist pregiven narratives about ourselves that are available to be "taken up"— especially those relating to social categories, such as race, ethnicity, age, sexual orientation, and gender, but also those concerning professional categories, such as doctors, lawyers, teachers, and so on.

As educators and change agents, we can interrogate these pregiven narratives. Reflexive narratives can be mobilized for this interrogation. These may awaken a capacity for agency and for self-determination—they offer a way of challenging and resisting dominant stories that are told about us. Education can play a major role in this regard. Certainly, marginalized groups, often supported through formal and informal education, have asserted and inserted new selves and new life stories into the mix of narratives circulating in the world. For example, Closson (2010) identifies "counterstory telling" as one of the five tenets of critical race theory. Mindful that critical race theory developed with a focus on legal scholarship, she asserts that the aim of counterstory telling is "to illuminate, by setting up a contrast, the majoritarian, race-neutral, and liberal meta-story in the law" (p. 176). Closson argues that the "race neutrality" or "color blindness" of the law functions to obscure disadvantage. Writing in a similar vein, Baumgartner (2010) draws attention to the different narratives that whites draw on to talk about race. In spite of good intentions, the narratives serve to entrench white privilege. She refers to the work of Hytten and Warren (2003), who identified a range of narratives used by whites to talk about race—for example, the discourse of "connection," in which whites empathize with black oppression by referencing their own oppression through homophobia or misogyny. Or there is the "enrich me" discourse, which trivializes racial issues by focusing on how whites can gain an enriching experience through exposure to indigenous or black cultures. Being aware of such narratives, challenging them in a reflexive way, and developing counternarratives are certainly crucial to having a meaningful dialogue concerning race in adult education.

It is clear that biographical narratives are not so much about individual lives as about how subjective experiences and unique life histories are linked to broader historical, social, and political circumstances, which have their own narratives. Constructing biographical narratives is also a means of inserting concrete lived experiences into various theoretical constructions of how we come to be formed as selves. Biographical narratives offer a technique and a method for analyzing lives, for linking up individual life stories to something more general—a holistic approach that integrates life stories, the social structure, narrative, and theory (see Plummer, 2001).

7

Knowing Oneself

Nearly all educational designs for personal change have a dimension of "knowing oneself." This may take various forms, such as examining one's worldview, assumptions, and paradigms; bringing to conscious awareness previously repressed or hidden feelings and thoughts; analyzing discrepancies between self-concept, self-esteem, and one's ideal self; revisiting one's biography or life story; seeing oneself anew through the eyes of others; or perhaps measuring oneself against established norms by undertaking psychological tests and completing psychological inventories. Typically the exercise of knowing oneself is used to establish the groundwork for personal change. For example, the purpose may be to reveal the self one has become—an undesired self, lacking in some respect; or the exercise may reveal a former, previously innocent and authentic self waiting to be unshackled and nurtured once more. Exactly what it is that comes to be "known" with self-knowledge and the route to self-knowledge is crucially important.

Ever since the ancient Greek maxim "Know thyself" was inscribed in the Temple of Apollo at Delphi, public figures from all walks of life—poets, philosophers, playwrights, novelists, priests, mystics, politicians, generals, psychiatrists, and others intent on imparting words of wisdom for living the good life— have all echoed the maxim in their own way. Some of their ideas are set out in Table 7.1, which includes quotes selected and edited (with additions) from a compilation available online as part of a leadership seminar titled "Here's Looking at You! The Know Yourself Seminar."

Table 7.1 Knowing Oneself—a Selection of Quotes from Antiquity to the Present

Socrates: I must first know myself, as the Delphian inscription says; to be curious about that which is not my concern, while I am still in ignorance of my own self, would be ridiculous.	Plato (423?–347 BCE), *Phaedrus*
No man is the worse for knowing the worst of himself.	Thomas Fuller (1654–1734)
Know then thyself, presume not God to scan / The proper study of Mankind is Man.	Alexander Pope (1688–1744), "An Essay on Man," Epistle II
The high peak of knowledge is perfect self-knowledge.	Richard of Saint-Victor (1120?–1173)
Self-knowledge called for severity, and I was always willing to go to the mat with that protean monster, the self, so there was hope for me.	Saul Bellow (1915–2005), *Ravelstein*
If most of us remain ignorant of ourselves, it is because self-knowledge is painful and we prefer the pleasures of illusion.	Aldous Huxley (1894–1963), *The Perennial Philosophy*
Study the heart and the mind of man, and begin with your own. Meditation and reflection must lay the foundation of that knowledge, but experience and practice must, and alone can, complete it.	Lord Chesterfield (1694–1773), letter to his son, June 6, 1751
Observe all men; thy self most.	Benjamin Franklin (1706–1790), *Poor Richard's Almanac*, 1740
And he who does not know himself does not know others, so it may be said with equal truth, that he who does not know others knows himself but very imperfectly.	Sir Joshua Reynolds (1723–1792), *Discourses on Art*, Discourse 7
Self-knowledge is the beginning of self-improvement.	Baltasar Gracián (1601–1658)
Self-awareness gives you the capacity to learn from your mistakes as well as your successes. It enables you to keep growing.	Larry Bossidy (1935–) and Ram Charan (1939–), *Execution: The Discipline of Getting Things Done*

Unless we can bear self-mortification, we shall not be able to carry self-examination to the necessary painful lengths. Without humility there can be no illuminating self-knowledge.	Arnold Toynbee (1889–1975), *A Study of History*
Ophelia: We know what we are, but know not what we may be.	William Shakespeare (1564–1616), *Hamlet*, 4.5.42
It's no good running a pig farm badly for thirty years while saying, "Really I was meant to be a ballet dancer." By that time, pigs will be your style.	Quentin Crisp (1908–1999)
We read books to find out who we are. What other people, real or imaginary, do and think and feel is an essential guide to our understanding of what we ourselves are and may become.	Ursula K. Le Guin (1929–)
Our greatest instrument for understanding the world—introspection. . . . The best way of knowing the inwardness of our neighbor is to know ourselves.	Walter Lippmann (1889–1974), *A Preface to Politics*
Everything that irritates us about others can lead us to an understanding of ourselves.	Carl Jung (1875–1961)
We do not grow absolutely, chronologically. We grow sometimes in one dimension, and not in another, unevenly. We grow partially. We are relative. We are mature in one realm, childish in another.	Anaïs Nin (1903–1977)

Source: Adapted from "Here's Looking," n.d.

It is not surprising that the quotes in Table 7.1, although united in their endorsement of self-knowledge, offer different reasons for seeking and routes to self-knowledge.

Facing Up to Yourself

One theme that emerges from Table 7.1 is the idea that embarking on a journey of self-knowledge, although worthwhile, is a struggle, and it may be necessary to face some "home truths" about yourself. This is evident in Saul Bellow's reference to the self as a "protean monster," Carl Jung's observation that what we find irritating in others is a good guide to what we may find irritating about ourselves, and Arnold Toynbee's warning about our capacity to bear the pain of self-examination.

Although self-knowledge is no doubt illuminating, it is worth posing the question of whether self-knowledge is always a positive thing. Is Thomas Fuller correct in saying that no person is worse for knowing the worst of himself or herself? Jung, for one, doubts whether this is true. In his autobiography *Memories, Dreams, Reflections*, Jung (1967) tells the story of a doctor who came to him for psychoanalytic training. He appeared to be completely normal in his work, family, and community life, and he requested Jung's assistance in becoming an analyst as an addition to his medical practice. Jung replied, "Do you know what that means? It means that you must first learn to know yourself. You yourself are the instrument. If you are not right, how can the patient be made right? . . . . [Y]ou must first accept an analysis of yourself" (p. 156). The doctor replied that he was willing to undergo analysis and advised Jung that he had no problems to tell him about. In retrospect, Jung observed that this should have been a warning sign. After analyzing the doctor's dreams, Jung identified what he termed a *latent psychosis*. In Jung's view this doctor could not have withstood analysis, and he terminated the training: "Immediately afterwards he returned home. He never again stirred up the unconscious. His emphatic normality reflected a personality which would not have been developed but simply shattered by a confrontation with the unconscious" (p. 158). This is a powerful story because it reminds us of the pitfalls in accepting the idea that self-knowledge is always a good thing for the person concerned. Self-delusion and self-deception obviously limit our capacity to live completely fulfilled lives, but they may nevertheless be necessary to continue to live normal lives. This observation also reminds us that most of the educational interventions in the name of self-knowledge are based on an ideal goal—the fully developed, aware, and conscious person—that may be unattainable for some. As Saul Bellow (2000) remarks, "Maybe an unexamined life is not worth living. But a man's examined life can make him wish he was dead" (p. 34).

Educators promoting personal change need to be mindful of the potentially negative consequences that can flow from self-awareness. One consequence may be that participants are traumatized by exercises designed to bring this awareness about. For example, one such exercise I have observed involves the use of guided imagery. Participants are asked to close their eyes and imagine they are floating in space. The facilitator prompts the imagination of participants with guiding questions, such as "What do you see?" and "How do you feel?" Participants are then invited to move toward earth, ever closer, until the details of earth are seen. "Can you see a river? How fast is it flowing? Dive into the river . . . is it warm or cold? What can you see in the water? How do you feel?" This kind of questioning continues until the facilitator brings participants back to a neutral place, the present, and asks them to open their eyes. Participants then share their experiences and feelings. This exercise is designed to promote the projection of internal feelings onto the external world. Handled skillfully this exercise is a very good introduction to the psychoanalytic concept of projection, and it can also lead to a greater degree of self-awareness. But handled badly or with vulnerable participants this exercise can lead to anxiety, or can reveal latent neuroses or even psychoses that may be best left alone or dealt with by a skilled psychotherapist or clinical psychologist. For this reason it is highly risky as an educational practice.

Self-Knowledge as an Ongoing Process

Another theme emerging from the quotes in Table 7.1 is that self-knowledge is always in process. This is so because self-knowledge is in the service of self-development; there can be no definitive knowledge of the self because the self is dynamic and always changing. And so self-knowledge must necessarily be about the past, which of course is always open to the vagaries of memory. Inga Clendinnen, in her pursuit of self-knowledge through her autobiographical work *Tiger's Eye* (2000), reveals her disquiet about her memories of childhood: "Writing my childhood made me see that the marshland between memory and invention is treacherous. . . . [W]hen I read my memories I am uneasy. I do not recognize the girl's temperament as continuous with mine. I don't think I was ever so competent. I think her competence may be an artifact of the writing. But it is also true that when I pulled her out from the rubble of time I discovered something about myself I had not known before" (pp. 73–74).

What Clendinnen discovered was a connection between her activities as a child (tickling trout in a river) and her subsequent interest in ethnographic history (touching something from a different world that is concealed and inaccessible, and searching for its shape, which is exactly the magic of doing history). This fragment demonstrates how we work on our experiences so they make sense—things are linked up that hitherto had gone unnoticed and not remarked upon. Making sense of our past experiences to better understand our desires and interests is a route to self-knowledge. It is for this reason that autobiographical analysis has emerged as one of the most widely used strategies in education. But what status should we give the meanings that we attach to our biographies? One approach is to assume that there is a single true biography for each person; another is to explore one's biography with a view to identifying multiple readings. Brookfield (1995) exemplifies the former approach in his reference to autobiography as one of the "four critically reflective lenses" through which we see the world. He uses autobiography in the context of teachers critically reflecting on their practices: "Analyzing our autobiographies as learners has important implications for how we teach. . . . [T]he insights and meanings we draw from these deep experiences are likely to have a profound and long-lasting influence. . . . [W]e may think we're teaching according to a widely accepted curricular or pedagogic model, only to find, on reflection, that the foundations of our practice have been laid in our autobiographies as learners" (p. 31).

The emphasis here is on autobiography as a foundation of practice. It is used to gain self-knowledge of one's commitments and beliefs as a teacher. In this instance, one's biography is something that is "unearthed": there is an accurate, true biography that is there to be discovered once the distortions and denials are unblocked. This is *very* different from the view that biography is always open to reinterpretation and re-authoring, as expressed in the practice of narrative therapy. In the former approach, self-understanding is promoted through an *accurate* account of one's biography. In the latter approach, self-understanding is promoted through opening up the possibility that one's biography can be rewritten (although, to be fair to Brookfield, he acknowledges being influenced by what he terms *pragmatic constructionism*, which stresses being open to possibilities; see Brookfield, 2009). But biographies are always constructions, and in such constructions self-deceit can be just as present as self-illumination. The key is to know the difference; but this knowledge is of course elusive, and it is by no means certain who holds to key.

Reflection on Experience

Another theme apparent in Table 7.1 is that experience is the foundation of who you are, as amusingly expressed by Quentin Crisp in his observation that after thirty years of pig farming, "Pigs will be your style." This implies that experience leaves an indelible mark on who we are and, given enough time, who we are capable of becoming. We are formed, however gradually, by our actions in, and on, the world, which is the Marxian notion referred to in Chapter Two. Marx of course was interested in how, under capitalism, workers become alienated from the products of their work, from the activities they undertake in the process of production, and ultimately from their own nature as human beings. He thus had a view of the intrinsic nature of humankind—"the fact that labor is *external* to the worker, i.e., it does not belong to his intrinsic nature; that in his work, therefore, he does not affirm himself but denies himself, does not feel content but unhappy, does not develop freely his physical and mental energy but mortifies his body and ruins his mind" (Marx, 1932/1993, p. 30).

This idea of the alienation of people from their work has resonated in academic and popular psychology throughout the twentieth century and to the present day. As mentioned in Chapter Two, alienation from work is typically portrayed as leading to alienation from one's authentic self. That is, our actions at work begin to form us in ways that are alienating and not true to our authentic nature. But it is not necessary to postulate the existence of an authentic self to be found beneath the surface— through our actions in the world we have simply become what we are. This implies that the route to self-knowledge is through an understanding of our actions and, more broadly, our practices in the world, as opposed to an understanding of our authentic nature. Reflection on action has a long history in education, but there are many different purposes and types of reflection as well as many different ways to conceive "actions" and "practices."

Reflection on practice has not hitherto been directed squarely at self-knowledge (see Le Cornu, 2009); it has mainly been used in the context of professional development, the development of a learning organization, or the kind of learning to be extracted from experience (see van Woerkom, 2010, for a recent review of these various applications of reflection). Nevertheless, the literature on reflection does have within it a general sensibility to the possibility of self-knowledge and self-development. For example, Dewey (1963), in writing about the role of experience in learning, refers to two principles. The first of these is the principle of continuity: "Every experience is a moving force. Its value can be judged only on the ground of what it moves toward and into" (p. 35). The second is the principle of interaction: "Every experience enacted and undergone modifies the one who acts and undergoes, while this modification affects, whether we wish it or not, the quality of subsequent experiences" (p. 35). Dewey was concerned here with the role of education in fostering continuous self-development through exposing learners to experiences of the kind that "live fruitfully and creatively in subsequent experiences" (p. 27). Dewey stops short, however, of inviting learners to reflect on how their experiences have changed or modified their understanding of who they are. This is not the case with Brookfield (2011), who regards critical reflection as the key to learning from experience. This involves four steps:

- The identification of the assumptions that frame our thoughts and actions
- The scrutiny of the accuracy and validity of these assumptions
- Viewing our thoughts and decisions from different perspectives
- Taking informed actions based on the thought and analysis in the first three steps

The recognition and analysis of assumptions are key to critical reflection. One technique for analyzing assumptions, the critical incident approach, is described by Brookfield (1991) in an earlier publication: "Learners are asked to produce richly detailed accounts of specific events and then move to a collaborative, inductive analysis of general elements embedded in these particular descriptions" (p. 181). The critical incident exercises that Brookfield devised follow a common pattern: the participants are asked to describe a concrete event that has triggered an emotional response, guided by questions such as "When?" "Where?" "Who was involved?" He then invites participants to identify the underlying assumptions informing their actions, which he describes as "those taken-for-granted ideas, commonsense beliefs, and self-evident rules of thumb that inform our thoughts and actions" (p. 177). Mezirow (1998), in his concept of transformative learning, also focuses on challenging everyday assumptions through critical reflection. Both Brookfield and Mezirow, and others who follow a similar path, have been criticized for being too rationalistic in their approach, perhaps because the very term *assumption* seems to signal the beginning of a rational argument. But this criticism is not really warranted, as both theorists refer to feelings and emotions in their exposition of critical reflection. Mezirow has this to say about reflection:

> Reflection, a "turning back" on experience, can mean many things: simple awareness of an object, event or state, including awareness of a perception, thought, feeling, disposition, intention, action, or of one's habits of doing these things. . . . Reflection does not necessarily imply making an assessment of what is being reflected upon, a distinction that differentiates it from critical reflection. . . . [W]e can become critically reflective of our own assumptions as well as those of others. Critical self-reflection of an assumption (CSRA) involves

critique of a premise upon which the learner has defined
a problem (e.g., "a woman's place is in the home," so I
must deny myself a career that I would love). Significant
personal and social transformations may result from this
kind of reflection [Mezirow, 1998, p. 185].

Critical self-reflection on assumptions involves exploring "canons, paradigms, or ideologies" and "norms, feelings, and dispositions" that frame and may constrain or limit our relationships and
how we see the world. The domains in which assumptions operate
include politics, bureaucracy, history, religion, linguistics, workplaces, communities, and families. In many ways this is quite similar to Freire's approach, which was adopted in literacy programs in
Brazil in the early 1960s. As outlined in Chapter Four, he sought
to develop among learners what he terms *conscientization*—a critical awareness of the self as a subject who can reflect and act on
the world in order to transform it.

   While teaching literacy he also sought to develop in learners a critical awareness of themselves—an ability to know themselves in the context of the circumstances in which they were
enmeshed. A drawing used by Freire in a literacy discussion group
or "culture circle" illustrates his approach. It depicts a hunter with
a bow and arrow shooting birds from the sky. The group began the
discussion by making a distinction between culture and nature
in the drawing. The participants came to think of the feathers of the bird as nature in some contexts and culture in other
contexts. While attached to the bird the feathers belong to the
world of nature; when the bird is killed and its feathers are used
as decorative headwear, they belong to the world of culture. The
culture circle discussed a variety of drawings such as these, always
with a view to elucidating how culture is created and transmit-
ted and how it can be changed. This may seem a long way from
the proposition that our actions and practices form us. However,
actions and practices are always carried out in the context of

an economic, political, and cultural framework, and it is the workings of this context at which critical reflection is aimed. Knowing yourself, then, is knowing how your actions and practices have been formed in a particular economic, political, and cultural framework. To borrow from Rose (1998), to know yourself is to know what this framework *does*—"what components of thought it connects up, what linkages it disavows, what it enables humans to imagine, to diagram, to hallucinate into existence, to assemble together: sexes with their gestures, ways of walking, of dressing, of dreaming, of desiring; families with their mommies, daddies, babies, their needs and their disappointments; curing machines with their doctors and patients, their organs and their pathologies; psychiatric machines with their reformatory architectures, their grids of diagnoses, their mechanics of intervention and their notions of cure" (pp. 178–179).

A route to self-knowledge, then, is to deconstruct the political, economic, and cultural frameworks in which we are embedded and "assembled" as selves.

Knowing Others as a Route to Self-Knowledge

A final theme concerns the relationship between knowing oneself and knowing others. In Table 7.1, Joshua Reynolds highlights the dialectical relationship between knowing yourself and knowing others: you must know yourself in order to know others, and you must know others in order to know yourself. Ursula K. Le Guin refers to how the knowledge of others leads us to knowing ourselves and, as important, to know what we may become. Walter Lippmann advocates the practice of introspection as a key to understanding the internal states of others. This is evident in the Diversity Workshop Survey on the following page, which has been used in a range of workplaces. Each of the questions requires introspection, but only in relation to others' perceptions, assumptions, views, and preconceptions. Typically this survey is presented to people at different levels of the organization (for example, board members, senior executives, middle managers, and office workers), with the percentage of "agree" or "disagree" plotted for each category of employment. This discussion can focus on a range of things, but participants are invited explicitly or implicitly to think of the flip side of each of these statements and ask of themselves, Do I behave in this way to others? With this approach self-knowledge is attained through applying to oneself those characteristics typically attributed to others. This is done in the context of a group discussion of the issues, which draws out the implications of the statements and the findings.

Diversity Workshop Survey

- I have been singled out as a representative of a particular group (for example, a work group) and asked to speak for that group.

- When I first met people in my group, I could see that they were talking to me or responding to me in a certain way because of assumptions they had made about who I was.

- Other people have been surprised when they have learned something about me that didn't fit their image of me.

- I have found myself saying or doing things to break out of other people's preconceived image of me.

- I sometimes have to explain to people how they have miscategorized me.

- Other people in this group make comments about me based on my race, gender, age, physical appearance, religion, occupation, clothes, or manner of speaking.

- I have felt that my ideas have not been taken seriously because of some category others have put me in.

- I sometimes feel frustrated because it seems that other people don't see me for who I really am.

- I am routinely excluded from certain activities because of assumptions others make about me.

Source: Adapted from Hateley and Schmidt, 2000.

In a similar way role plays and simulations invite participants to project their own thoughts and feelings into a prescribed scenario. In a sense this is self-exploration through the mask of the "other," which may be more revealing than direct methods of self-examination, such as introspection. Many role plays and simulations are designed to foster self-knowledge in the debriefing stage through an analysis of how we carry out our roles. A classic simulation that is widely used is Bafa Bafa (Shirts, 2009), in which participants are assigned to one of two very different cultures: Alpha, which is a relationship-focused culture that values physical closeness and is not competitive, and Beta, which is a highly competitive trading culture. There are a set of rules to follow for each culture in carrying out an activity, such as playing cards. In Alpha culture the rules are only enforced by women, and include "standing close together," "maintaining continuous eye contact while talking," "touching with the pointer finger as a greeting," and "flapping your arms as a sign of respect for taller people." In Beta culture the rules include "never making physical contact, and keeping three feet away from others," "never making eye contact when talking with someone," "touching your own nose as a form of greeting," "showing off and bragging," and "saying, 'Oh yeah' as a sign of respect for shorter people." It is clear that when these two cultures come together to perform a task, there is considerable misunderstanding of the others' intentions. For example, Alphans will not respond to Betans who attempt to talk with them without first touching them. Although the simulation is based on a highly structured set of rules, the outcomes are more open-ended, with such debriefing questions as "What did you learn about yourself and others by participating in this simulation?" In this instance the simulation format allows participants to experience "otherness" in a way that is designed to be nonthreatening.

The educational and psychological literature is replete with techniques, processes, and practices for "knowing oneself," which is seen as a necessary condition for personal change. Whether we approach this task through our unconscious, our biography, our actions in the world, or our ways of relating to others, self-knowledge always comprises an analytic, cognitive dimension and some kind of emotional engagement. For some the emotional dimension is experienced as a form of enlightenment or spirituality, in which the relation of self to self is transformed. The reflexive, shifting nature of the self suggests that it is futile to attempt to know oneself in any complete sense. All we can hope for with self-knowledge is to capture fragments or moments of that elusive sense of our own enduring psychological continuity.

8

Controlling Oneself

The work of "self on self" implies some degree of agency and control. Invariably, self-knowledge is not sufficient for personal change. It is also necessary to act on those things that work against personal change in order to sustain it, such as everyday habits; patterns of interpersonal relationships; community and organizational structures in which one is embedded; and broader social structures and agencies that oppress, deny, or overly shape who you are. Many designs for learning foster mastery and the exercise of authority over oneself. That is, self-regulation, self-monitoring, and self-discipline, which may take such forms as personal goal setting, time management, daily planning, or practicing a regime of habits or exercises.

Self-control is understood here as a conscious effort to carry out or avoid certain actions and emotional states. As such it is similar to the concepts of self-regulation and self-discipline. Baumeister and Alquist (2009) address the important question of whether self-control is a good thing. They note that there are general social and individual benefits arising from self-control, arguing that the benefits of ordered social life are only made possible through a level of self-control among its members: "Self-control enables individuals to fit in to societies and to navigate their way through the myriad constraints and opportunities society presents. The self-control of individuals also enables social systems to operate smoothly and serve their functions, because self-controlling individuals obey the society's rules and perform their roles within it" (Baumeister and Alquist, p. 117).

This echoes Freud's view that ordered social life depends on the control of instinctual impulses. Indeed there is now empirical support for the view that self-control as a human trait is related to such positive life outcomes as school achievement; more secure and satisfying relationships; and a reduced incidence of depression, addiction, eating disorders, and even psychoticism (Tangney, Baumeister, and Boone, 2004). But Baumeister and Alquist (2009) are also mindful of the costs of self-control. They argue that where self-control requires an effort, the subsequent depletion of energy leads to a diminished capacity for ongoing self-control and a diminished functioning in other areas that depend on the same energy, such as logical reasoning, decision making, and taking initiative. In addition, self-control can lead to reduced emotional sensitivity, less spontaneity, and less openness to new experiences. And so self-control is a mixed blessing—it has both an upside and a downside—and therefore needs to be managed carefully. Having said this, it is worth considering some of the basic approaches to self-control.

Delayed Gratification

Having the capacity for delayed gratification is seen as a developmental milestone in the growing child. This is a cognitive as much as an emotional development in the sense that it is predicated on the prior capacity to distinguish between the present and the future state of affairs, to anticipate a future, and to see the future on a time continuum—near, short term, middle term, and long term. A classic test of delayed gratification is the "marshmallow test," whereby four-year-old children were asked to choose between an immediate reward, one marshmallow, and a delayed reward of greater value in twenty minutes, three marshmallows. Those who resisted the temptation to take the smaller but immediate reward in order to secure a larger reward were seen to have better self-control (see Shoda, Mischel, and Peake, 1990, for a follow-up study). Wulfert et al. (2002) used a similar technique in their study of delayed gratification among adolescents. They invited students to participate in a survey of academic achievement and substance abuse, but their real interest was in measuring the students' capacity for delayed gratification and correlating this with academic achievement, self-esteem, and various measures of problem behaviors. Participants were given a choice of receiving either an immediate payment of seven dollars for their participation or a one-week-delayed payment of ten dollars. Those who chose to select the seven dollars immediately (approximately 50 percent of the students) were seen by the authors as exhibiting a "failure to delay gratification" (p. 540).

In these standard psychological experiments the choice to delay gratification is seen as a mature response to a conflict between immediate temptation and long-term goals. It is a mature response in the sense that it rests on the capacity to separate long-term personal interests from short-term personal interests, an ability to assess the likelihood of long-term interests' being realized, and an ability to project one's thoughts into a future state of affairs in which your interests are being met. From an educational point of view a capacity for delayed gratification is paramount because learning is effortful and demands concentration and application—it is not always fun and entertaining as some would like to believe, and the outcomes and benefits of learning are not always evident in the short term. Learning requires an act of faith in the future and a wider framework for resisting temptation.

Strategies for Resisting Temptation

Self-control normally comes into play when there is a conflict between realizing our long-term, or broader goals, and the satisfaction of our immediate desires. We face these conflicts daily, such as when the temptation to join friends on a night out conflicts with a longer-term goal to complete an assignment or finish preparation for a work presentation, or when the invitation to join others at a bar conflicts with a scheduled exercise class linked to a longer-term goal of a healthy lifestyle. Temptations and conflicts occur across a range of human activities, such as dieting, giving up smoking, or self-managing a chronic illness. There is always the temptation to do those things one ought not to do, and not to do the things one ought to do, in order to achieve long-term goals. Fishbach and Converse (2010) identify approaches to overcome these temptations. They argue that the first step is to identify the conflict. In order to do this we need to identify our actions with both "width" and "consistency." By using the term *width*, they mean framing the present temptation not as a single, isolated opportunity, but in the context of a range of other opportunities. "The person who says 'one jelly donut won't kill me,' perceives the temptation in isolation, notes that there are trivial costs associated with eating it, and likely does not experience a conflict between this breakfast and his more important health goals" (pp. 245–246). However, if this action is seen in the context of a planned new morning routine, then a self-control conflict is more likely to be identified. They argue for the efficacy of using a wide frame for comparing opportunities. By using the term *consistency*, they mean that the person concerned should expect the present decision to be replayed in the future. If eating the donut is seen as a "one-off" or special exemption, then it is unlikely to lead to conflict. If it is seen as setting a precedent for the future, a conflict will be identified.

They illustrate these strategies by referring to one of their studies in which they set up a free food stand on a university campus. The stand had both healthy food (such as carrots) and unhealthy food (such as chocolates). When the sign for the stand read, "Spring Food Stand" (the wide-frame condition), student customers consumed fewer chocolates and more carrots. When the sign for the stand was changed to "April 12th Food Stand" (the narrow-frame condition), the student customers consumed more chocolates and fewer carrots. Thus narrow framing of a low-cost temptation, such as by calling it a "special occasion," does not lead to conflict, and therefore temptation triumphs. Wide framing, however, leads to the identification of a conflict. Fishbach and Converse have tabulated a range of strategies that can be successfully used to resist temptation. These are reproduced in a slightly modified form in Table 8.1.

The overall approach for resisting temptation is to strengthen the motivation to achieve higher-order goals and weaken the motivation to give in to lower-order temptations. As can be seen from Table 8.1, there are two overarching strategies. The first strategy is to modulate the choice situation. This can be done through a precommitment to forgo, self-imposed penalties, or avoidance. A precommitment to forgo means anticipating a conflict in advance and making a prior commitment to forgo temptation and to pursue goals. For example, a person who has set a goal to improve her health may make a commitment to a one-hour walk immediately following the day's work. This may well

Table 8.1   Self-Control Strategies Directed at the Motivational Strength of Goals and Temptations

Strategies	Temptations	Goals
Modulating the choice situation	Precommitment to forgo Self-imposed penalties Avoidance	Precommitment to pursue Self-imposed rewards Approach
Modulating the psychological value of choice options	Inhibiting Devaluing Setting low expectations Cool and abstract construal	Activating Bolstering Setting high expectations Hot and concrete construal

Source: Adapted from Fishbach and Converse, 2010, p. 248.

conflict with the desire to "wind down" with a few drinks at home or with colleagues. Anticipating this conflict in advance and making a precommitment strengthen the likelihood of resisting temptation. Generally speaking, the anticipation of strong temptation increases self-control efforts. Another method relates to the formulation of self-imposed penalties and rewards (for example, allowing yourself to undertake a desired recreational pursuit once you have completed an onerous task; or, conversely, denying yourself such recreation if you fail to complete the onerous task). Indeed there is now a popular self-control tool that is available at www.stickk.com. A final method is avoidance—you anticipate and plan to avoid situations in which the conflict may occur. For example, a person wanting to give up smoking may identify situations in which the triggers to smoke are very strong—such as when playing cards or drinking at a bar. These situations can be avoided, and the costs of avoidance (for example, social isolation) can be counteracted by identifying alternative activities.

The second overarching strategy is to modulate the value of choice options—that is, to work directly on the strength of your motivations. This may involve inhibiting thoughts about temptations, perhaps by thinking negatively about the consequences of giving in to temptation while consciously focusing on goals. It is also possible to think negatively about the value of the temptation and more positively about the value of the goal. For example, "That chocolate looks a bit rich to me," "That bread is too salty for my tastes," or "I liked the way I felt after the long walk yesterday." Fishbach and Converse (2010) also provide experimental evidence of the efficacy of developing a distant, abstract, "cool" attitude to the temptation. Finally, developing an optimistic attitude that you will be successful in pursuing valued goals and resisting temptation has also been found to have positive effects. That is, if you have a low expectation of giving in to temptation and a high expectation of pursuing your goals, you are more likely to resist temptation.

The paradigmatic research on self-regulation sets up a conflict among participants between short-term, tempting, but deleterious choices, and long-term, positive goals, as in the case of overcoming addiction or managing one's diet for health reasons. However, long-term goals may themselves be incompatible and work against each other. For example, career goals may conflict with family life goals; the pursuit of a vocation that is not well remunerated (for example, fringe theater) may conflict with financial goals; or the goal of living in a foreign land and learning a new language may conflict with the goal of being a caregiver for an elderly parent. Pursing one positive goal over another is not usually labeled as a temptation, but the psychological dynamic is similar—it requires self-control to eschew a choice, even if that choice is framed as a positive goal rather than as a negative temptation. This points to the importance of how we come to set our goals and prioritize them, which has a lot to do with how we see and understand ourselves.

A further point needs to be made: the discussion so far has centered on self-control and avoiding temptation in relation to choices or actions, but there is another type of self-control that has been well documented: emotional control (see Gross, 2007, for a review of the research). Koole, van Dillen, and Sheppes (2010) outline some strategies for "downregulating" an unwanted emotion. These strategies include avoiding the situation in which the emotion is triggered; deploying your focus away from the object of the emotion (for example, by engaging in demanding work or strenuous physical exercise); cognitively reappraising the situation (for example, by seeing it from the point of view of a detached observer); and modulating the behavioral and physiological expression of the emotion (for example, by using controlled breathing and muscle relaxation). An example of the last type of strategy is integrated body-mind training (Tang and Posner, 2009), which uses body relaxation, mental imagery, music, and breathing adjustment to achieve a balanced state of relaxation and focused attention. Another example is the mindfulness meditation training of Kabat-Zinn (1991), referred to in Chapter Nine on taking care of oneself. These types of strategies are not very far removed from the strategies advocated in the self-help literature, to which I now turn.

Popular Self-Help Literature and Self-Control

In addition to the contribution of academic psychology to understanding and strategizing self-control, the popular self-help literature has numerous examples of how to control oneself to sustain fundamental change—and it does not shy away from emotion and the analysis of broader life goals. My interest in the self-help literature is not to advocate its techniques, but to draw attention to the assumptions it makes about people and their capacity for change, and to contrast their approach with the transformative learning approach discussed in Chapter Three. One of the most popular self-help texts is Stephen R. Covey's work, *The 7 Habits of Highly Effective People* (1989) which centers on the practice of daily habits built on such injunctions as "be proactive," "begin with the end in mind," "put first things first," "think win-win," "seek first to understand, then to be understood," "synergize," and so on. It is through the practice of these habits that self-awareness and self-mastery are achieved, and so Covey spends a great deal of his book providing his readers with the tools to diagnose and correct their negative habits, and the motivation to adopt and practice new, more positive habits. For example, with respect to his first habit, he implores us to "listen to our language," and he provides examples of "reactive" and "proactive" language (see Table 8.2).

Covey proceeds to provide tasks, strategies, and actions to help inculcate all seven habits in those reading his book. His approach to self-control, which entails the everyday practice of habits, is the second of three elements in his approach to personal change, which is

- A strengthening of the motivation for change, normally by stressing the ways in which we live our lives according to the expectations and scripts of others, together with the promise of a more fulfilling life if we can overcome these expectations

- The understanding that personal change is driven by the commitment to practicing everyday habits, which are ultimately "character forming"

- A singular view of the desirable end point of self-change—the autonomous, choosing individual

Table 8.2   Reactive and Proactive Language

Reactive Language	Proactive Language
"There's nothing I can do."	"Let's look at our alternatives."
"That's just the way I am."	"I can choose a different approach."
"They won't allow that."	"I can create an effective presentation."
"I have to do that."	"I will choose an appropriate response."

Source: Adapted from Covey, 1989, p. 78.

Anthony Robbins adopts a similar approach in *Awaken the Giant Within* (1992). He focuses on changing behavioral habits through the process of neuro-associative conditioning. Neuro-associative conditioning has six steps (pp. 124–145):

1. Decide what you really want and what's preventing you from having it now.

2. Get leverage: associate massive pain to not changing it now and massive pleasure to the experience of changing now!

3. Interrupt the limiting pattern.

4. Create a new, empowering alternative.

5. Condition the new pattern until it's consistent.

6. Test it!

An excerpt from his fifth step illustrates the flavor of his approach: "If you rehearse the new, empowering alternative again and again with tremendous emotional intensity, you'll carve out a pathway, and with even more repetition and emotion, it will become a part of your habitual behavior. Remember, your brain can't tell the difference between something you vividly imagine and something you actually experience" (Robbins, 1992, p. 137). Like Covey, he recognizes the power of language in personal transformation, and many of his exercises are based on building a new personal vocabulary by replacing old, negative words with new, positive words. This is well illustrated in the chapter "The Vocabulary of Ultimate Success," in which he reminds us, "Remember that your brain loves anything that gets you out of pain and into pleasure, so pick a word that you'll want to use in place of the old, limiting one" (p. 216). An excerpt from his list of possible positive replacement words and their negative counterparts is shown in Table 8.3.

Robbins also develops exercises for promoting the ongoing monitoring of progress. In one such exercise he asks readers to allocate a score and a short description to each of ten critical areas of life: "physically," "mentally," "emotionally,"

Table 8.3   From Negative to Positive Emotion

Negative Emotion/Expression: "I'm Feeling . . ."	Transforms into: "I'm Feeling . . ."
Anxious	Expectant
Dread	Challenge
Failure	Learning
Lazy	Storing energy
Lost	Searching
Fearful	Curious
Stressed	Energised

Source: Selected from Robbins, 1992, pp. 216–218.

"relationships," "attractiveness," "living environment," "socially," "spiritually," "career," and "financially" (Robbins, 1992, p. 277). His instructions for this exercise are as follows: "Next to each of these categories, give yourself a score on a scale from 0 to 10, 0 meaning you had nothing in this area, and 10 meaning you were absolutely living your life's desire in that category. . . . [W]rite a sentence next to each category to describe what you were like back then [five years ago]" (p. 276). Robbins asks readers to do this exercise for *yesterday* (five years ago), *today*, and *tomorrow* (five years in the future), with an instruction to reflect on what has been learned by the comparison.

In his chapter "Creating a Compelling Future," Robbins invites readers to identify their personal, career, material, and "contribution" goals. He prompts readers to visualize a better future by asking questions about their personal goals, such as "What would you want to learn? . . . Study the violin with virtuoso Itzak Perlman?"; "What do you want to earn? . . . $10 million a year?"; "What would you like to purchase? . . . A private zoo stocked with giraffes, alligators, and hippos?"; "How could you contribute [that is, to the lives of others and to society]? . . . Read to the blind? . . . Halt the destruction of rainforests? . . . Eliminate racial discrimination?" (Robbins, pp. 290–300).

Robbins uses these questions to raise the issue of the kind of person one needs to become in order to realize his or her goals. He asks readers to write a paragraph describing all the character traits, skills, abilities, attitudes, and beliefs they would need to develop in order to achieve all of their goals (see p. 303). In summary, Robbins's approach to personal change requires visualizing a better future, substituting new behaviors for old, and undertaking personal strategic planning. For him, to know oneself is to know the limiting patterns and thought processes that have hitherto prevented personal fulfillment. Knowing oneself in this way leads to a renunciation of these patterns and the pursuit of a regime of behavior and language focusing on goals that are more fulfilling.

An important practice in knowing oneself is writing, which functions to help the writer renounce past patterns of living and identify and embrace goals for the future. Robbins's position is that we are in control of our self-change, we have a high degree of individual autonomy and agency, and we can use this to achieve whatever goals we set.

The self-help literature has been criticized for producing the opposite of what it claims to achieve, largely because of its focus on individual psychology and its failure to consider the social context. Rimke (2000) takes up this theme in her application of a Foucauldian framework to her analysis of self-help texts:

> Popular psychology's unilateral focus on individuals contributes to a worldview which erroneously postulates that people can exercise control and mastery of themselves and their lives. Self-help literature, which exalts the individual over the social (and negates the inherent sociality of being) is elaborately consistent with the political rationalities promoted in advanced liberal democracies. Self-help literature aids in the production, organization, dissemination and implementation of particular liberal modes of truth about the social world. The discursive production of "self-helping citizens" is an effect of discourse naturalizing itself and thereby rendering psychological subjects as natural self-governing objects in a (pre)discursive world [Rimke, 2000, p. 62].

She argues that the self-help literature constitutes a contemporary form of governing citizens. She is using "government" in the Foucauldian sense of all those regimes (tactics, strategies, calculations, reflections, and programs) that function to "conduct the conduct" of individuals. The self-help literature is one such regime, and "self-helpers" are thus agents in their own subjection to authority. This is a well-worn line of argument for those who follow the Foucauldian opus. As outlined in Chapter One, it has been applied more broadly to psychology as a discipline, and not only to the popular self-help texts (see Rose, 1998). But it is not necessary to take on the entirety of this argument to see that it has some merit and that caution needs to be exercised in any practice that intervenes in the name of the self. The mainstream transformative learning literature recognizes this and is very conscious of the limits of controlling oneself: "Acquiring greater control of one's life as a liberated learner is, of course, always limited by social, historical and cultural conditions" (Mezirow, 2000, p. 27).

Whereas the self-help literature tends to focus on the ongoing need to "control oneself" in daily routines, the transformative learning literature tends to focus on the transformation of meaning perspectives, or frames of reference, that have their own "habits of mind." "Self-control" is to be found in being vigilant through ongoing reflective practice on the personal, work, community, social, economic, and political conditions in which you live. And so an important aspect of self-control is planning changes to those conditions and how they affect you. This may involve committed political action, community engagement, establishing a new set of interpersonal relationships, negotiating work redesign or new work tasks, and challenging "languaging" practices that position you or others in unfavorable or demeaning ways. These can be seen as "higher-order" interventions compared to those daily practices recommended in self-help texts. Nevertheless, "controlling oneself" is a feature of most transformative learning designs, the purpose being to act in some way in order to sustain transformational change. Whether this action is directed inwardly or outwardly, or whether it is "higher-order" or "lower-order," there is a requirement to implement new strategies for relating to self and others as well as to consciously practice new behaviors and attitudes.

9

Caring for Oneself

This chapter has its origins in my reading of Foucault's essay "Technologies of the Self," which appears in an edited book of the same title (Martin, Gutman, and Hutton, 1988). In this essay Foucault traces the development of technologies of the self in Greco-Roman philosophy and in early Christianity. Technologies of the self, which stand alongside and interact with technologies of production, sign systems, and power, "permit individuals to effect by their own means or with the help of others a certain number of operations on their own bodies and souls, thoughts, conduct and way of being, so as to transform themselves in order to attain a certain state of happiness, purity, wisdom, perfection, or immortality" (Foucault, 1988b, p. 18). Foucault is particularly concerned with the notion of "taking care of oneself" as a precept or imperative that circulated among a number of different doctrines in the period from 3 BCE to 3 AD. This is a theme developed more extensively in the third volume of *The History of Sexuality*, which is titled *Care of the Self*. In this text, Foucault refers to the time and effort expended in attending to oneself in antiquity:

> Taking care of oneself is not a rest cure. There is the care of the body to consider, health regimens, physical exercises without overexertion, the carefully measured satisfaction of needs. There are the meditations, the readings, the notes one takes on books or on the conversations one has heard, notes that one reads again later, the recollection of truths that one knows already

but that need to be more fully adapted to one's own life. . . . There are also the talks that one has with a confidant, with friends, with a guide or director. Add to this the correspondence in which one reveals the state of one's soul, solicits advice, gives advice to anyone who needs it. . . . Around the care of the self there developed an entire activity of speaking and writing in which the work of oneself on oneself and communication with others were linked together [Foucault, 1988a, p. 51].

Foucault analyzes the techniques associated with different doctrines concerned with the care of the self, from the practices of Stoic teachers, such as holding spiritual retreats, meditating, practicing ritual purification, and mentoring, to the Christian tradition of confession, disclosure, and renunciation of the self. Many of these techniques are in use today, on occasion in their original form but often appearing in a new guise as educational practices.

Taking Care During the Passage of Change

Metaphors of healing are often invoked in the literature on education for personal change, particularly in what is known as transformative learning (Mezirow, 2009). Many writers focus on the emotional, intuitive, extrarational, and intensely personal aspects of transformational change (see Dirkx, 1997; Scott, 1997; Cranton, 2000; McWhinney and Markos, 2003). In these instances learning designs incorporate such elements as confessional practices, cathartic experiences, and the exploration of personal relationships at home and in the workplace. Practices used for this purpose may be writing letters to oneself; diary writing; exploring self-image and values; experiencing guided imagery; documenting critical life events or incidents; journaling; exploring one's life history; and examining one's own needs (emotional, intellectual, social, and spiritual)—often through expressive activities, such as drama or art. McWhinney and Markos explore what they term the "archetypal form of transformative education . . . of death and rebirth, of regression in the service of a forward leap" (p. 16). They illustrate transformative learning through the Navajo Indian healing ritual with its stages of "crisis and retreat," "entry into the womb of the earth" (the liminal space), the "transformative passage," and "reintegration or rebirth" into daily life. The liminal space is interesting because it is marked by a symbolic death of the self, which has parallels in contemporary practices: "In current day ceremonies (often in growth workshops), separation begins with obscuring one's name and professional identity, dumping one's life story so that one's baggage will not block self-awareness or inhibit talk with others. The resulting nakedness allows everyone to join in creating a community of searchers and be open to instruction by a mentor. Without identity, intimacy becomes tolerable and attractive" (McWhinney and Markos, p. 26).

This is interesting because none of the conceptions of the relationship between self and society hitherto discussed would allow conscious entry into such a "selfless" state as a possibility. This would require, in one fell swoop, the conscious elimination of the impact of distortion, oppression, language, social forces, and interpersonal relationships on shaping and defining the self. This implies a level of personal agency and autonomy well beyond what most believe is possible. Yet there are many practices that attempt to induce such a state, and it must be acknowledged that many people report experiencing such a state, especially when it is supported by engagement with a new community and physical isolation from everyday activities.

DeGloma (2008) documents what he calls "awakening narratives"—stories of those who have "seen the light" or "woken up" to the truth about themselves or the world and have therefore undergone a significant life change: "Awakenings describe a major metamorphosis of consciousness that is aptly captured by the metaphor of the cocoon. Just like you cannot teach a child that a caterpillar and butterfly are the 'same' being without describing the cocoon, we can not explain such major transformations of mind without reference to an awakening experience. The awakening experience marks a cognitive turning point in the awakener's life story and justifies the transformation of the awakener's worldview" (p. 21). Examples of awakenings include the changes wrought through recovered memories of childhood sexual abuse, the changed consciousness of veterans who have returned from deployment, religious conversion, the discovery of sexual identity, the transformation of political consciousness, and overcoming alcoholism. The form of the awakening narrative is similar across these different types of awakenings. There is a temporal distinction between truth and falsehood, accompanied by a divided self—the past self is characterized as being lost, in darkness, blind, and false; the present self is "found," in the light, sighted, and true. This form of the awakening narrative is the same whether a person is moving into or away from a religion, or whether he or she is recounting a recovered memory or recanting a previously recovered memory. DeGloma writes, "The awakening episode is thus wedged in a space of narrated liminality, in between past and present as well as darkness and light. The awakening experience gives meaning to both past and present, structuring the distinction between truth and falsehood" (p. 21).

When an awakener talks about his or her past self it is as if it were another person. The significant thing about such awakenings is that denying the past self also entails denying the community in which that self was located. The awakener becomes estranged, if not ostracized, from his or her old community. This is illustrated by a Mormon apostate who comments in the Recovery from Mormonism forum:

> For those of us who have Mormon family, they don't support us at all. Hell, most of us who had Mormon friends [they] dumped us, because we're suddenly

too evil to be around. Suddenly, all of the people you depended on and care about tell you that you're the scum of the earth and they don't want anything to do with you, or they insist you conform. Intolerance continues . . . until it is unbearable.

[The Recovery Forum is] not support to stop attending church, it's support to fill in for the "friends" [notably, in quotes] and family who dumped us cold because they are intolerant enough to view us as evil [quoted in DeGloma, 2008, p. 19].

The need for self-care is evident in the accounts of personal change of the magnitude described by DeGloma (2008). In the ex-Mormon's account, self-care takes the form of finding a new community that provides support. This is not just support for the new worldview—it is support in dealing with the rejection of the "old" community. As DeGloma notes, awakeners are both apostates and converts: apostates because they are typically rejecting former beliefs and the affiliations that go with those beliefs, and converts because they are adopting new affiliations and have available to them the comfort and security of like-minded others. But in a sense the very form of the narrative of awakeners also provides an example of self-care: the narrative of distancing oneself from "past selves" shifts the locus of responsibility and accountability onto another person—the person with whom you no longer identify. Thus the narrative does the work of self-care, "as the awakener simultaneously separates and joins, rejects and embraces, mourns and celebrates" (DeGloma, p. 18).

Meditation as an Exemplar Self-Care Practice

Another more consciously adopted technique for taking care of oneself is meditation, a practice that has recently being analyzed by Newman (2008). In this chapter I will take Newman's analysis as a case study to discuss the issues arising from meditation as a self-care practice. In doing so I acknowledge that meditation is closely linked to a variety of spiritual traditions, some of which encourage meditation from a theistic perspective (see Tisdell, 2008).

Newman (2008) gives an account of his experience in a meditation program in Sydney, his participation being motivated by a desire to support his wife, who was participating as part of her management of an aggressive form of cancer. He is keen to point out that he saw the meditation not as some kind of cure for cancer but as a way of supporting his wife's depleted immune system and bolstering her psychological state. The meditation was based on a form of mindfulness as developed by Kabat-Zinn (1991) and colleagues at the University of Massachusetts Medical Center. The program was initially used for pain management, but its application was broadened to include stress reduction and the promotion of a sense of well-being. The approach was secular, even though its origin in Buddhist religion was acknowledged. Newman explains the notion of mindfulness:

> Mindfulness is developed by paying attention purposely and nonjudgmentally to what is going on in the body and the mind in the present moment. Rather than dwelling on the past or anticipating the future, the meditator seeks to develop a moment-to-moment awareness of the here and the now. This is done through a range of focused physical and mental exercises. . . . We were introduced to the idea of doing the most banal of everyday things, such as eating a raisin, attentively. We were guided through exercises that made us scan our bodies and focus on our breathing. We were taught certain positions and movements taken from different forms of yoga. We were taught to walk mindfully and to sit, relaxed and motionless [Newman, 2008, p. 285].

Newman pays particular attention to the all-day intensive, in which the participants were required to remain silent and avoid eye contact and communicating by gesture. He then goes on to express his doubts concerning the whole program. These doubts take the form of Marxian doubt, Dialectical doubt, Absurd doubt, and Moral doubt.

Marxian doubt focuses on the origin of our consciousness: "I do unquestioningly subscribe to the idea that we generate our consciousness in relationship with our social and material worlds. Our consciousness is not a given but has to be created through our actions in and on our world" (Newman, 2008, p. 287). This is referred to as Marxian doubt because it was Marx above all who advanced the proposition that consciousness is determined by social being (see Marx, 1932/1993). If such a proposition is accepted, then it is clearly at odds with any practices that require separation, social exclusion, and isolation in the name of developing consciousness of the self. Newman argues, quite rightly (accepting the Marxian proposition), that if participants fail to examine their engagement in the outside world and their relationships within it, then in a sense their selves will be diminished rather than augmented and they will be less rather than more conscious.

Dialectical doubt is portrayed in relation to the ongoing dialectic between self and world—or self and others, if you like. Each term of the dialectic has no meaning without its opposite because it is the relationship that is center stage: "Take my world, take the people and things surrounding me, away, and my concept of self has no meaning. The self ceases to exist. On that Sunday in the Sydney program, in silence, without interaction, and with reflection confined to a concentration on the moment and the breath in that moment, I felt I was denying the relationships upon which my self relied. If I blocked out the world, I necessarily blocked out the self as well. Instead of sustaining my sense of self, I was negating it" (Newman, 2008, p. 289). For Newman, self-care is about the interaction between self and others—it is with others that we learn and grow and heal—it is not a matter of looking inward but one of looking outward. In this respect the care of the self is also about the care of others, or at least the care of the self in relation to others. I should emphasize here that Newman subtitles his article "A Rationalist Meditates," but it is not only his rational being that is affronted by techniques that involve looking inward in isolation from others—his experience is a strong, emotional sense of loss of self.

Absurd doubt has to do with the existentialist notion of "absurdity"—the freedom to search for meaning in an ultimately meaningless world. In the meditation exercise there was no attempt to give meaning to thoughts, sensations, or feelings. Newman argues that the focus on the self in meditation distracts us from the responsibility to act in the world—that is, to change ourselves through changing the circumstances in which we live. Newman provides the example of a work stress-reduction program that focuses only on the individual management of stress but fails to address the root causes of stress in the workplace.

Finally, Moral doubt starts from the assumption that happiness and well-being are dependent on some kind of social order, which invariably means some kind of moral order. Thus morality is a social concept created in the company of others that entails a judgment of "right" and "wrong." In the isolation of meditation, however, there is an injunction to be nonjudgmental:

> We were told to be nonjudgmental of our thoughts and emotions, and again I found the instruction contradictory. If I am to relate to myself and not to a shadow of myself, then I must understand the self as a feeling, thinking, and therefore moral entity. I must assess my thinking and feeling against my conscience. I cannot note a thought without asking, "Why do I think like that?" I cannot note a feeling without asking, "Why do

I feel like this?" I may look into myself in a compassion-
ate, kindly, and intimate manner, but I must do it with
judgment.

Questions of conscience require me to examine my
position in the material and social worlds. They require
me to make judgments, adopt positions, and take sides.
They require me to approve and disapprove [Newman,
2008, p. 291].

Newman extends his doubts about meditation to doubts about the
broader field of experiential learning interventions in the name of
the self, such as those of Mezirow (2000); Cranton (2006); Boud,
Cohen, and Walker (1993); and Rogers (1983). For example, he
argues that some experiential learning designs explicitly set out to
create a moral free zone: "Such conditions can provide the opportunity for some people to do and say reprehensible things, while
inhibiting others from protesting at what has been said and done.
In the interests of a spurious kind of self-development, we adopt
a nonjudgmental position. We abandon our responsibilities to
construct and apply a moral code, and so cease being fully human
ourselves. We abandon our responsibility to bring people to book
either in the confines of the program or, if necessary, outside it"
(Newman, 2008, p. 292).

An example that comes to mind here is the values clarifica-
tion exercise I witnessed, which involved a hypothetical post-
apocalyptic scenario whereby the survivors of a nuclear holocaust
were asked to choose their fellow survivors from among a list of
potential people with defined characteristics (for example, young
female, young male, doctor, engineer, and so on). This was a well-
known exercise at the time and it was used extensively in the
period when antinuclear marches were at their peak in Western
countries. The problem with this exercise is that it asks students
to suspend their disbelief and accept what turned out to be out-
rageous for some of them—that survival and the possibility of a

renewed life were actually possible after a global nuclear war. In some respects it was fortunate that partway into the exercise a small group refused to continue; a lively discussion ensued (with some painful exchanges), and the exercise was abandoned for another less-controversial scenario.

And so Newman (2008) argues strongly for the kinds of interventions that are genuinely based on engagement with others, engagement with the circumstances in which we live, and engagement with a strong foundational moral purpose. But Newman goes too far in claiming that self-care is meaningless without these elements. To take Marxian doubt first, although it may be true that our consciousness is brought into being in relation to others and the material world, once formed our consciousness can have a relationship with itself; that is, consciousness is *reflexive*. As Kierkegaard observed, "The self is a relation which relates itself to its own self" (quoted in Neville, 1996, p. 204). Arguably, moreover, the relationship of self to self is also (paradoxically) dialectical in the sense that the self, through reflection, can be an agent of its own change. On the issue of Moral doubt, Sundararajan (2008), in her critique of the positive psychology movement and its apparent scientific neutrality, agrees with Newman on the necessity of a moral map, but her solution is diametrically opposed to his: "It is questionable whether any form of life that is considered 'good' can be devoid of a moral map. . . . [S]elf-reflexivity constitutes a so far neglected intrapersonal dimension. . . . [A]t the level of individual consciousness, self-reflexivity can render our moral maps visible, articulate, transformative, and in turn amenable to transformation" (p. 656). For example, it is only through inward attention that we can evaluate our desires and emotional responses. I would add that reflexive consciousness is necessary to question, challenge, and, if necessary, change the moral maps governing our lives.

Finally, on the question of Absurd doubt, Newman (2008) argues that the meaninglessness of life puts the onus back on us to create our own meaning. Of the meditation exercise he says: "The challenge was there to give meaning to our thoughts, feelings, and sensations but we did not. We let our thoughts, feelings, and sensations be and returned to our breathing. We were free to act but we did not. . . . [W]e have a responsibility to make use of that freedom, and it could be argued that a focus on the self discourages us from taking up that precious responsibility" (p. 290). But one could argue the opposite, that care of the self through meditation and its focus on detachment and savoring provides not only a source of meaning but also a renewed readiness for action. As Sundararajan (2008) points out, savoring, which involves inward attention to the senses and the thing in itself, endows experiences with meaning. In the context of the kind of illness that motivated Newman's participation in meditation, it can also be "a response in terms of acceptance, but not resignation; letting be, but not giving up; savoring rather than coping" (Sundararajan, pp. 669–670). I am not suggesting here that detachment, isolation, and an inward gaze should dominate our lives, but rather that these can provide a respite from unhealthy attachments, a life of busyness and distraction, and a constant outward, action-oriented focus.

Self-Reflexivity and Care for Others

Nelson Mandela provides testimony to the value of isolation and detachment, albeit enforced in his case. While in prison on Robben Island he wrote the following to Winnie Mandela (also in prison) on February 1, 1975:

> Incidentally you may find that the cell is an ideal place
> to learn to know yourself, to search realistically and
> regularly the process of your own mind and feelings.
> In judging our progress as individuals, we tend to con-
> centrate on external factors such as one's social posi-
> tion, influence and popularity, wealth and standard of

education. These are, of course, important in measuring one's success in material matters and it is perfectly understandable if many people exert themselves mainly to achieve all these. But internal factors may be even more crucial in assessing one's development as a human being. . . . At least if nothing else, the cell gives you the opportunity to look daily into your entire conduct, to overcome the bad and develop whatever is good in you. Regular meditation can be very fruitful in this regard [Mandela, 2010].

This extract comes from a book titled *Conversations with Myself*, which speaks volumes for the benefits of self-reflexivity as a practice in taking care of oneself in circumstances in which the ability to act has been circumscribed. Newman's doubts about meditation and the broader field of experiential education are worth raising, and there is certainly a need to be mindful of the dangers of exclusively inward-looking practices in education and the care of the self. However, his doubts can be allayed by recognizing, as did Mandela, that the care of the self is not a "selfish," "amoral" activity, but an activity central to connections with others and to actions in the world that are founded on a moral purpose.

I should acknowledge here the importance for self-care of caring for others—especially in situations such as those experienced by Mandela. Caring for others can take the form of caring for individuals, groups, communities, nation-states, or humanity more generally. This is evident in the testimony of Liu Xiaobo, recipient of the 2010 Nobel Prize for Peace and jailed dissident. After explaining that he bore no hatred for the police, prosecutors, and judges involved in his arrest, interrogation, prosecution, and sentencing, at the People's Intermediate Court in Beijing on December 23, 2009, he made this statement: "Hatred is corrosive of a person's wisdom and conscience; the mentality of enmity can poison a nation's spirit, instigate brutal life-and-death struggles, destroy a society's tolerance and humanity, and block a nation's progress to freedom and democracy. I hope therefore to be able to transcend my personal vicissitudes in understanding the development of the state and changes in society, to counter the hostility of the regime with the best of intentions, and defuse hate with love" ("Liu Xiaobo's Final Testimony," 2010, p. 19).

Liu goes on to link his personal love with his aspirations for the state:

> Ask me what has been my most fortunate experience of the past two decades, and I'd say it was gaining the selfless love of my wife, Liu Xia. . . . Your love is sunlight that transcends prison walls and bars, stroking every inch of my skin, warming my every cell, letting me maintain my inner calm, magnanimous and bright, so that every minute in prison is full of meaning. . . . Even if I am crushed into powder, I will embrace you with the ashes.
>
> Given your love, my sweetheart, I would face my forthcoming trial calmly, with no regrets about my choice and looking forward to tomorrow. I look forward to my country being a land of free expression, where all citizens' speeches are treated the same; where different values, ideas, beliefs, [and] political views . . . both compete with each other and coexist peacefully ["Liu Xiaobo's Final Testimony," 2010, p. 19].

Here Liu gives a powerful account of where the meaning in his life is located. It is not in thinking about himself, but in his attachments to others. He is not pursuing self-care as a goal in its own right, but a consequence of his caring for others is that he is taking care of himself in the best way possible, given his circumstances.

10

(Re)creating Oneself

Franz Kafka, writing in the early years of the twentieth century, produced two compelling tales about personal transformation and change. The best known of these, *The Metamorphosis*, begins with the sudden and unexpected transformation of the principal character, Gregor Samsa: "When Gregor Samsa awoke one morning from troubled dreams he found himself transformed in his bed into a monstrous insect" (Kafka, 1915/1996). Gregor, although understandably shocked and confused, tries initially to keep things much the same as any other morning, thinking about everyday things like the irritations of his work and the need to rise early. He seems as much preoccupied by his failure to hear his alarm and his subsequent lateness for work as he is with his newly transformed appearance. Focusing back on his condition, he decides to hide himself away in his room, but when he eventually opens the door to his family and a work colleague they immediately pull back in disgust and fear. The story proceeds through the initial sympathies and consolatory gestures of this family to their outright rejection of him and his ultimate death. The story is moving because Gregor is essentially unchanged from a psychological point of view—his identity is intact—but he is now grotesquely distorted. His attempts to communicate with his family are misinterpreted and rejected. He is like so many people in our world who lead marginal lives. And it is a story about the tragedy of such lives because of the treatment meted out by others. The other tale was published as "A Report to an Academy" (Kafka, 1948/1995) but has recently been dramatized as "Kafka's Monkey." It comprises a talk by a monkey named Red Peter to a learned academy in Britain in the late nineteenth century. This particular monkey had learned to read and write and gives an account of his transformation from a wild jungle animal to the kind of "person" who could give an articulate account of his experiences in the presence of men of letters and science. He describes how he was shot and captured and held in a cage in the bowels of a ship on his way to England. He decided that the only way to survive was to imitate the gestures, manners, and speech of his captors. As he explains, he was completely content as a monkey and he had no desire to take on all these human attributes—he did so only in order to survive, and survive he does. This tale brings to mind the transport to Europe of specimens of indigenous peoples from the Pacific, Australia, Africa, and the Americas. In many instances such people took on the manners and dress of Europeans, much like how Red Peter takes on human qualities. Like *The Metamorphosis*, this is a tale about the treatment given to those who are "other." But it is also a tale about the resilience of identity in the face of substantial outward change. The tragedy for Gregor Samsa is that he could not articulate the continuity of his identity in the face of such a massive change in appearance. The tragedy for Red Peter is that he had to live a lie—to appear to be different in order to survive. Both have in common the experience of marginality.

Change at the Margins of Life

Musgrove (1977), in an early treatment of the experience of marginality, reports on seven ethnographic case studies of change in adult life that focus on groups of people who occupy extreme, strange, or abnormal positions in society. He asks how it is that consciousness comes to be modified by the experience of marginality. Two of his case studies analyze involuntary and unwelcome change: that experienced by those who have become disabled and by those who have become blind. The remaining case studies analyze voluntary change among late entrants to the Anglican ministry, members of a Sufi commune, self-employed artists, Hare Krishna converts, and members of gay communities. Of the involuntarily marginal groups Musgrove observes:

> The blind and the residents of the Cheshire homes are remarkable for the persistence and continuity of their self-perceptions over many years and even decades of extreme and grievous "marginality." Finding new recipe knowledge does not necessarily sustain a new reality: it supports and even strengthens the old.
>
> The studies also disabuse us of the simplistic view that some social psychologists hold that assuming new "roles" means creating a new self. All the people in this study had moved to a new status and a new role, but "real selves" often remained latent though undimmed and available for recall. . . . [E]xtreme marginality does not lead easily and automatically to the dissolution of an established self and a fundamentally reconstructed reality [Musgrove, pp. 14–15].

Thus members of involuntarily marginalized and stigmatized groups (such as the paralyzed and the blind) maintain their respective historical identities in the face of the changed gaze of others—just like Kafka's Gregor Samsa. And then there are the legions of people who, like Red Peter, play out roles in family and working life to then return to their "real selves" when those roles are no longer required to be enacted—for example, employees who spend a lifetime being publicly compliant with, but privately resistant to, organizational demands on their values, attitudes, and practices; parents who spend twenty years or more raising children; and, in Musgrove's study (1977), artists who have "their 'real selves' disinterred after fifty years of camouflage" (p. 14). And then there are those members of the gay community who "come out": "The shame that I had when I 'came out' was in telling my friends who thought they knew me. They didn't know me at all. And so what a lying relationship it had been. I'd posed as the arch-hetero. . . . But suddenly to be known for yourself—it's the most exciting thing you can imagine" (quoted in Musgrove, p. 34). This person's psychological identity had not changed at all, but rather was illuminated for others to see, and this required courage and a series of negotiations with his fiancée, with close friends, and with his parents. Thus he was engaged in a particular type of change: he needed to change his relationships with others and locate himself differently in the world.

Finally, in Musgrove's case studies there are those who do fashion new selves, such as the members of Sufi and Hare Krishna communes. Both the Sufis and Hare Krishnas use ritual and ceremony to symbolize transition and change, such as cleansing before meditation to wash away one's former self, providing offerings of incense and conch shells, and ritualistic dancing. They enter a world of routines and rules, chanting and meditation, fasting and praying, studying and working. The conversion is often sudden, following a period of liminality in which life is uncertain, ambiguous, and unsatisfactory. As a member of the Sufi community testifies, "I was into a really heavy scene: drugs, rock music, a bit of radical politics. I must have been insane, all that nonsense. . . . [T]hen I just happened to run into the devotees one day and I've never looked back. It took me a while to surrender completely, but you know there's nothing so completely satisfying" (quoted in Musgrove, p. 207). Another devotee observes, "They sort of take all your ideas away, everything you think, and smash them all up. They're really merciless. You feel terrible. But at the same time you feel foundation stones going down for something else, something better" (quoted in Musgrove, p. 208).

Musgrove's observations are supported by McWhinney and Markos (2003). As described in Chapter Nine, they analyze the transformative journey evident in Navajo Indian healing rites. In their article they invite a broader perspective on transformative learning, they see the entry into the liminal space as the beginning of transformation: "On entry one experiences a symbolic death of the existing self. One way or another, crossing the threshold separates the participants from normal activity and expectations, as would their bodily death. They move into a liminal domain that is nowhere, those who cross the threshold vanish from their familiar selves" (p. 26).

Change in Everyday Life

Musgrove's analysis (1977) was informed by the sociological theory at the time, specifically Berger's social constructionism (1963). He also adopted a particular methodology—ethnography—to provide a detailed account of particular instances of change. In all cases those involved in change were depicted as marginal. But is the process of change the same for those who identify with the mainstream? What are the dynamics of successful change for those experiencing commonplace life changes? Heatherton and Nichols (1994) provide some answers to such questions, using a psychological and quantitative approach as opposed to the sociological and qualitative approach adopted by Musgrove. They set out to document the reasons for successful as opposed to failed attempts at life change. Half of the 119 participants in their study were asked to recount an instance in which they had made a successful major change, and the other half were asked to recount an instance of desired but unsuccessful change. The stories of actual and desired changes fell into clear themes: career, education, relationships, addictive behaviors, health behaviors (including diet), and attitudes toward life (changes in perspective or personality). As it turned out these themes were divided evenly between the successful and failed change stories. In writing their stories the participants were asked to explain the reasons for the successful change or the factors preventing change. The authors were thus interested in the question, To what did the participants attribute their success (in the case of changers) or failure (in the case of non-changers)? The results were grouped into six categories (Heatherton and Nichols):

- Control—including self-control in general, control over specific behaviors, accepting responsibility, and external barriers to change

- Focal events—including external threats, critical incidents, stories about others, religious conversion experiences, and the importance of religion in general

- Emotional aspects—including changes from negative to positive affect, everyday difficulties and frustrations, strong negative emotions, and major suffering

- Interpersonal aspects—including others' requesting change, seeking and receiving help, social support, comments from others about behavior, and others' commenting about change or received benefits

- Methods used—including preparation for change, the use of educational materials, consideration of alternative methods, the use of a public declaration, taking steps to alter the immediate environment, moving to a new location, thought control, and the use of self-reward techniques

- Meaning and identity issues—including sudden flashes of insight, the crystallization of discontent, a reappraisal of goals, an increase in self-knowledge and understanding, clinging to a former role, and being ambivalent about change

As you might expect, the changers reported more control, both over the specific behavior and in general. Non-changers blamed external barriers as preventing their control and were less likely to take responsibility for their change attempt. External threats (to health, well-being, and happiness) were important for both groups, although the changers mentioned them more often. Changers were also more likely to mention a focal event or critical incident that initiated change. The critical incident was often something that happened to someone else—an accident or an instance in which someone else had made a similar change. Both groups reported daily hassles as important, but changers were more likely to mention extreme negative emotions—allayed by the positive emotions associated with success. On all the interpersonal elements the changers were more engaged with others in the change process. In terms of the methods used, changers and non-changers prepared for change equally. The main difference in this category is that changers were much more likely to alter the environment, either by moving or by changing aspects of the immediate environment. A low percentage used forms of thought control, such as meditation and relaxation, and there was not a significant difference between the two groups. The only group to use self-reward techniques was the changers, albeit at a low level. Perhaps the greatest difference between the two groups can be found in the meaning and identity issues category. The changers reported a greater increase in self-knowledge and awareness and a clearer capacity to pinpoint their discontent (for detailed results, see Heatherton and Nichols, 1994, p. 668). The authors emphasize the importance of identity change as a means to sustain behavioral change: "This change in identity incorporates the changed behavior so that the previous behavior is no longer viewed as part of the self. . . . The new identity clearly helps the changed person sustain the motivation to change. Claiming to have undergone a complete change in identity enables the person to associate the changed behavior or situation with the previous version of self, not with the new version of self: the 'old me' used to do this, but the 'new me' does not. The person brackets off the behavior as reflective of the past and not predictive of the future" (Heatherton and Nichols, p. 672).

This study reveals some key elements of change: the crystallization of discontent, perhaps through some focal event or external threat; the recruitment of significant others in initiating and sustaining change; the importance of changes in the external environment; and conceiving of the change in terms of a new identity and increased self-knowledge.

Positive Psychology and Change

A more contemporary approach to personal change is evident in the positive psychology movement. The millennial issue of *American Psychologist* was devoted to articles on positive psychology, which focuses on positive subjective experiences, positive human traits, and positive institutions. Titles of articles in the special issue (see Seligman and Csikszentmihalyi, 2000a) include "The Evolution of Happiness," "Subjective Well-Being," "The Future of Optimism," "Wisdom," "States of Excellence," and "Creativity and Giftedness." Proponents of positive psychology see themselves as countering the dominant paradigm of psychological theory and research—a paradigm based on such human psychological pathologies as neuroticism, anxiety, and psychoticism. As such they are part of an earlier lineage of psychologists who have sought to focus on health and well-being, most notably Rogers (1951); Maslow (1954, 1968); Jahoda (1958); Erikson (1963, 1982); and Vaillant (1977). The project of positive psychology is explained by the editors of the special issue in this way: "The field of positive psychology at the subjective level is about valued subjective experiences: well-being, contentment, and satisfaction (in the past); hope and optimism (for the future); and flow and happiness (in the present). At the individual level, it is about positive individual traits: the capacity for love and vocation, courage, interpersonal skill, aesthetic sensibility, perseverance, forgiveness, originality, future mindedness, spirituality, high talent, and wisdom. At the group level, it is about the civic virtues and the institutions that move individuals toward better citizenship: responsibility, nurturance, altruism, civility, moderation, tolerance and the work ethic" (Seligman and Csikszentmihalyi, 2000b, p. 5).

In many ways the positive psychology movement can be seen as the more academically respectable side of the self-help movement, the aim being to understand and assist people to lead fulfilling lives—to create a positive self with positive psychological qualities. This appears to be a worthwhile project, and so we must ask, What practices do they advocate, and how do they conceive of the self and its capacity for positive change? As far as practices go, Seligman et al. (2005) have undertaken an empirical investigation of a range of interventions aimed at increasing happiness and life satisfaction. The interventions they used were distilled from a range of practices from Buddhism, the human potential movement, and the self-improvement industry. These formed the basis of one of six "happiness exercises" undertaken by participants in a randomized control study to measure the effects of the interventions on two measures: one on depression (the Beck Depression Inventory) and one on happiness (the Steen Happiness Index). The exercises included one placebo activity (journaling for one week about early memories), an exercise on building gratitude, two exercises that identified the positive aspects of oneself, and two exercises that focused on strengths of character. These are presented in Table 10.1.

The authors reported that three of the exercises resulted in increased happiness symptoms and decreased depressive symptoms for one to six months (exercises 2, 3, and 5 in Table 10.1). The other exercises resulted in transient positive effects only (exercises 4 and 6). The authors see this experiment as evidence of the potential to intervene in people's lives to reduce depression and increase happiness. My interest is not so much in the details of

Table 10.1   Interventions to Improve Happiness

Intervention	Description
1. Placebo control exercise: early memories	Participants were asked to write about their early memories every night for one week.
2. Gratitude visit	Participants were given one week to write and then deliver a letter of gratitude to someone who had been especially kind to them but had never been properly thanked.
3. Three good things in life	Participants were asked to write down three things that went well each day and their causes every night for one week. In addition, they were asked to provide a causal explanation for each good thing.
4. You at your best	Participants were asked to write about a time when they were at their best and then to reflect on the personal strengths displayed in the story. They were told to review their story once every day for a week and to reflect on the strengths they had identified.
5. Using signature strengths in a new way	Participants were asked to take our inventory of character strengths online at www.authentichappiness.org and to receive individualized feedback about their top five ("signature") strengths (Peterson, Park, and Seligman, 2005). They were then asked to use one of these top strengths in a new and different way every day for one week.
6. Identifying signature strengths	This exercise was a truncated version of the one just described, without the instruction to use signature strengths in new ways. Participants were asked to take the survey, to note their five highest strengths, and to use them more often during the next week.

Source: Selected from Seligman et al., 2005, p. 416.

the results but in the whole project of positive psychology and its assumptions about the self and how it can change.

The problematic aspects of positive psychology have been the subject of a special issue of *Theory and Psychology* (Christopher, Richardson, and Slife, 2008). A key article sets out the ontological underpinnings of positive psychology and offers an alternative approach (Slife and Richardson, 2008). The authors see the project of positive psychology as having fundamental flaws deriving from three of its features: a commitment to "disinterested observation," the importance placed on emotional satisfaction, and the tendency to see the self as decontextualized. The key idea underlying the "disinterested observer" is the separation and independence of the observer from the world being observed. This view presumes that the human agent or self is a highly individualized, abstracted, and detached observer of a world that is quite separate from the observer and his or her observations: "This approach is 'disinterested' because it denies that it incorporates any particular cultural aims or moral values while writing its own particular cultural biases into the nature of things" (Slife and Richardson, p. 706). The disinterested observer is morally and ethically neutral, which leads to a very individualized and instrumentalist ethics, one in which the person seeks the good life and obtains as many pleasures or "payoffs" as possible—satisfying self-defined goals and promoting personal well-being. There is no room here for an ethical and moral position that takes community and social life as its centerpiece. The alternative to disinterested observation, argue Slife and Richardson, is engaged agency:

> Long before a person takes a stand on one side or another of an issue, he or she has been deeply socialized in terms of what questions, assumptions, or dimensions of meaning are important and define those issues. Those assumptions and meanings inter-define us and link us together in profound ways.

We can (and often should) allow them to be called into question, leading to a shift in our goals and directions [for] living. But we can never question or stand apart from all such assumptions at once, in what could only be a bewildering vacuum. Rather, we must take for granted many of them as a basis for any questioning or critique when that seems needed [Slife and Richardson, p. 709].

Slife and Richardson (2008) argue that the second feature of positive psychology—the focus on emotional satisfaction—is open to the charge of pure egoism with no place for such values as self-restraint, sacrifice, and moderation: "Humans do not simply desire particular outcomes or satisfactions in living. Rather, they also make 'strong evaluations' of their desires. . . . Even if only tacitly or unconsciously, they evaluate the quality of their desires and motivations and the worth of the ends they seek in terms of how they fit their developing overall sense of a decent or worthwhile life. Without a perspective of this sort it simply is not possible to make sense out of the many secular reformers who give their lives for the liberty of future generations or the many parents who make sacrifices for their children" (p. 713). The problem for positive psychologists is that they strongly distinguish the objective realm from the subjective realm. And so when they look for moral and ethical principles they can either look toward the established authority and traditions for rules and precepts regarding the good life (the objective realm), or they can look to the subjective realm—what is good is what "feels" good for you. The relational alternative is to see the objective and subjective realms as interpenetrating. In the relational alternative the good life is realized in and through relationships with others: "Our relatively outward practices and institutions and our relatively inward meanings and values flow into one another in a holistic life-world. In this realm of praxis, our shared meanings and values are just as much 'out there' in our practices and institutions as 'in here' in our thoughts and feelings about outer events" (Slife and Richardson, p. 714).

The third feature of positive psychology is that it conceives of the self as decontextualized. That is, the qualities we exhibit exist independently of the context into which they are applied. But it makes no sense to be "cheerful," "optimistic," or "full of gratitude" outside of any context to which these qualities are applied. Similarly it is difficult to conceive of attitudes and values, principles, and even philosophies as only abstractions, devoid of any context. They only have meaning within a context. The authors pose a relational alternative as recognizing that

> the most fundamental and real entities of the world are the contextually situated aspects of our experiences, practices, and actions. In this view, the subjective cannot be divorced from the objective, and our histories, culture, and physical surroundings have to be taken into account when deliberating about a flourishing life or its qualities. This is not to say that ethical principles and value systems are unimportant or do not play a crucial role in human affairs. Rather, it is to claim that these abstractions must be validly derived from and always related to the concrete particulars of the contexts in which they occur [Slife and Richardson, 2008, p. 717].

The three features of positive psychology just dealt with—the disinterested observer, the focus on emotional satisfaction, and the decontextualized view of the self, have their origins in an epistemology that gives precedence to the abstract over the concrete, and to the atomistic over the holistic. Can the same be said of the plethora of learning designs that can be and have been used for personal change?

Learning Designs for Personal Change

McWhinney and Markos (2003) remark, "Every design [for transformative learning] implies a theory of human and social development, and every design has a political effect on the participants, whether by implication or by following an explicit ideology" (p. 27). A good way to test this view is to analyze the learning designs that can be found in texts that include activities for teaching to promote personal change. One such text is *Developing Adult Learners* (Taylor, Marienau, and Fiddler, 2000), which describes over seventy activities used by adult educators that attempt to change the attitudes, beliefs, and behaviors of adults through drawing on their experiences and reflections on experiences. Some examples of activities are listed here (with the authors of the designs listed in parentheses):

- Perspective shift (Munaker), the purpose of which is to introduce a strategy for an individual or members of the group to "stand above" or outside both their rational and intuitive selves and to help a learner tap his or her tacit knowledge (p. 112)

- Discovering true perceptions (Morton), the purpose of which is to increase awareness of one's perceptions and views of life and to assess what may be "holding one back" (p. 110)

- Symbols circle (Hicks), the purpose of which is "to help individuals define, own, name, and claim their own experience; and to challenge the larger worldview while shoring up their own" (p. 103)

- Examining your paradigms (Proehl), the purpose of which is "to recognize the power of paradigms in guiding thoughts and patterns, examine one's paradigms that affect attitudes and work values, and share with others one's basic assumptions or paradigms about work" (p. 120)

- Repertory Grids (Candy), the purpose of which is "to raise to the level of awareness for conscious analysis of those assumptions toward greater self-understanding" (p. 50)

- Contradictions workshop (Dunn), the purpose of which is "to discern and name the underlying patterns, structures, or limiting beliefs in the present circumstances—that is, the *contradictions*, that block a group's vision—so that strategic, corrective action might be taken" (p. 56)

- Educational autobiographies (Clark and Kilgore), the purpose of which is "to encourage learners to identify and reflect on specific life events, in this case, educational experiences; construct a cohesive interpretation of those experiences in an integrated way . . . [and] critically assess their own interpretations" (p. 69)

The activities in the preceding list vary from learning involving the administration of highly structured psychological and learning instruments (for example, the Repertory Grid, the Myers-Briggs Type Indicator, the Kolb Learning Style Inventory, and the Hemispheric Preference Scale) to more unstructured learning that involves sharing experiences relating to such themes as blockages to one's vision, the unearthing of tacit knowledge, or the bringing together of cognitive and affective modes of operating. Similar approaches are apparent in other volumes, such as *Challenges of Practice: Transformative Learning in Action* (Wiessner, Meyer, and Fuller, 2000), which describes a range of learning activities designed to explore attitudes and values relating to areas including antiracism, drug offender education, the control of violence, urban reform, small businesses, workplaces, the arts, and spiritual and personal transformation. Further examples of learning designs can be found in Mezirow and Associates' *Learning as Transformation* (2000), and Mezirow, Taylor, and Associates' *Transformative Learning in Practice* (2009). Commenting on this last publication, Newman (2010) questions whether the educational activities proffered constitute opportunities for fundamental personal change:

> Despite the title, many of the case studies that appear in *Transformative Learning in Practice* (Mezirow et al., 2009) are simply examples of good adult education practice. Brookfield (2009) describes a workshop in which, using an inventive array of exercises, he encourages people from the corporate world to critically examine dominant ideologies, but nowhere does he suggest that they leave their jobs. Some of the case studies are examples of introspective teaching and learning. Elizabeth Tisdell (Tisdell and Tolliver, 2009) describes how she encourages students to analyze the cultural messages they have internalized, but nowhere does she suggest that the students should, or could, abandon one cultural background for another [Newman, 2010, p. 10].

Newman seems to think that without direct action, fundamental personal change has not occurred. This of course is a moot point, and to be fair to Brookfield, he does link critically reflective learning in the workplace to action concerning worker cooperatives, cooperative democracy, and worker control (see Brookfield and Holst, 2011, p. 37). Leaving aside the necessity for action as the defining criterion for fundamental personal change, it is possible to discern common threads in the apparent diversity of activities: the discovery of a deeper or truer self; the development of a more unified and coherent identity; the development of a more integrated self; and, of particular importance, the development of a self that is transformed through a change in the assumptions, perceptions, or paradigms (that is, the "lens" or "model") through which one views the world. These features echo those of positive psychology in that it is the abstracted, autonomous self that stands apart from the world and analyzes and evaluates this world through an individualized lens. The limitations of the metaphors of the internal model or internal lens for understanding self-change have already been covered in Chapter Six, in which I quoted Gergen and Kaye (1993), who, in a manner similar to Slife and Richardson (2008), proposed a relational view of the self as an alternative to these metaphors. But what are the implications of adopting a relational view of the self?

The implications can be illustrated with reference to a particular pedagogical tool: critical self-reflection. One immediate implication is that there is no necessity to search, through critical self-reflection, for an invariant or definitive narrative. Quite the contrary, it would be overly rigid and prescriptive to develop a singular narrative that simply replaces an earlier, more dysfunctional narrative. A relational view of the self sees singular narratives as restraining and limiting our capacity to explore different relationships. The emphasis instead is on the generation and exploration of a multiplicity of meanings. This involves a form of pedagogy that opens up different ways of punctuating experience, explores multiple perspectives, and endorses their coexistence. Such a pedagogy enables learners to construct things from different viewpoints, releasing them from the burden of developing a limiting, singular narrative of the self. Learners can then be free to

> find exceptions to their predominating experience; to view themselves as prisoners of a culturally inculcated story they did not create; to imagine how they might relate their experience to different people in their lives; to consider what response they might invite via

their interactional proclivities; to relate what they imagine to be the experience of others close to them; to consider how they would experience their lives if they operated from different assumptions—how they might act, what resources they could call upon in different contexts; what new solutions might emerge; and to recall precepts once believed, but now jettisoned [Gergen and Kaye, 1993, p. 258].

On first glance this appears to be strikingly similar to existing practices in "critical reflection" as exemplified by Brookfield (2005) in his use of autobiographical critical reflection, described in Chapter Three. But in Brookfield's scenario the emphasis at the outset is on discovery rather than creation: the questions posed are, "Who am I?" and "Have I got it right?" Thus his approach can be seen as a secular version of the "confession." In a case of religious conversion, confession is followed first by renunciation and then by the affirmation of a new faith and the practices it entails. The practice of critical reflection, and many other contemporary transformative learning designs, are arguably secular versions of this road to Damascus—critical self-disclosure is followed by a form of renunciation (for example, "I renounce the way I have been the mouthpiece for an oppressive ideology," or "I renounce the way I have been narrated in the world"), and then by a commitment to a new replacement narrative. The alternative is to ask different kinds of questions, such as "Is this rendering of experience desirable?" and "What relationships can be invented or modulated through such a rendering of experience?" It is these questions that are posed when adopting a relational view of the self. Although the teaching techniques are similar on the surface (for example, exploring alternative interpretations with other teachers and learners), the whole project is fundamentally different. For example, in exploring our identities as teachers, the task is not to "discover" and problematize "who we are" or "how we are positioned" in terms of race, gender, class, sexual orientation, or ableness, but rather to explore multiple stories within each of these categories with a view to opening up new relations of power and authority (see Tisdell, 1998, for a slightly different treatment of positionality in poststructuralist feminist pedagogy). Thus a relational view of the self implies a pedagogy of self-reflection that insists not on discovering who one is but on creating who one might become.

A good starting point for developing a pedagogical model for this approach can be gleaned from the interventions in narrative therapy, particularly the use of "externalizing conversations," as outlined in Chapter Six, which explore past experiences and identify "counterinstances" to the dominant interpretation of past events. The use of externalizing conversations ensures that the problem being addressed is not internalized and psychologized (as in the confession) but rather externalized and *socialized*. The problem is seen as something governing the person through taken-for-granted practices related to particular modes of life and thought. The identification of counterinstances—events from the past when the problem was thwarted—helps build a sense of personal agency. Counterinstances provide the raw material for re-authoring the self and opening up different and multiple readings of past experiences. Thus the seeds of the "new" self are to be found in the "old." Indeed the practice of family therapy, in which White (1989) developed much of this narrative approach, has long advocated what is referred to as an "integrative approach." The integrative approach involves the use of a range of techniques combined with a "respect for the multiplicity of truths" (Nichols and Schwartz, 2004, p. 348), whereby no one theory or model is applied in its entirety to the exclusion of others. This is more than mere eclecticism, which just focuses in a pragmatic way on the techniques that seem to work. It is the use of multiple theories and multiple practices in combination.

Larner (2010) illustrates this in his treatment of Tom, who is depressed and suicidal:

> Tom is trapped within a self-constructed wall of silence feeling all the more desperate for it. From this *psycho-dynamic* stance of the counter transference I take in and think of Tom's emotional pain and his struggle with depression and secrecy. This reverie inspired me to talk in a *psychoeducational* way about the incidence of depression, suicidal thinking and self-harm in the adolescent population. I attempt to normalize his experience and reassure him suicidal thinking in young people is not uncommon and nothing to be ashamed about. In a *cognitive* therapy way I then explore and challenge Tom's beliefs and reasons for remaining secretive about his suicidality. Next from a *narrative therapy* perspective I refer to the importance of exposing suicidal thinking, explaining [that] like a virus it traps you into keeping its secret, which increases its power. I suggest the best disarming strategy is to confide in others and with my colleague stress the importance of doing this, right now, with his Dad in a *systemic family interview*, which explores their relational bonding [Larner, 2010, p. 309].

Larner moves freely between different therapeutic languages, integrating his training in psychoanalysis, cognitive therapy, and family therapy; his clinical intuition and experience; his bureaucratic responsibility to implement protocols for managing suicidal risk; and his acquaintance with the evidence-based literature for adolescent depression. Concurrently he works from a position of *not knowing*—maintaining an openness through being curious, flexible, and responsive in the therapeutic relationship. This requires what he describes as a combination of an ethic of hospitality *and* an irreverent stance toward different therapeutic languages (Larner, 2003, 2010).

The version of the self underlying this integrative approach is both autonomous and heteronomous, multiple and singular, independent and dependent, coherent and fragmented, stable and volatile. These may appear to be mutually exclusive qualities, but only if we see the self as somehow *complete*. However, the self can never be known in any complete sense, partly because our reflexivity (our ability to think about ourselves and our thoughts) leads in principle to an infinite regression, and partly because we are always changing, partial, and fragmented. Given this, how is it possible to re-create ourselves? The answer surely lies in our *engaged agency*—although we cannot completely stand outside our culture, we do have the capacity to question its assumptions and premises. And although it is certainly the case that our selves are forged and sustained within a culture, we all have unique biographies and unique predispositions and potentials. This is the source of our independence and our capacity for agency—to act in the world, to engage in debate about moral and ethical issues, to challenge prevailing practices, and to manifest for ourselves changes in how we relate to others and ultimately ourselves. Those of us engaged in interventions in the name of personal change need to cast a critical eye on our own practices and their rationale, particularly if we wish to avoid inadvertently propping up a version of selfhood that is highly individualized, stable, and separated from the social. In doing so we need to be open to different theoretical ideas and practices, to have an irreverent stance toward different theories, but at the same time to have an ethic of hospitality. The question is not Has this theory got it right? but rather Does this theory open up different ways of rendering experience—ways that prove to be useful for promoting learning in the name of change?

References

"Adoptee and Birth Parent Reunion Stories." Adopting.org, n.d. www.adopting .org/reunions.html.

Alfred, M. "Challenging Racism Through Post-Colonial Discourse: A Critical Approach to Adult Education Pedagogy." In V. Sheared et al. (eds.), *The Handbook of Race and Adult Education: A Resource for Dialogue on Racism.* San Francisco: Jossey-Bass, 2010, 201–216.

Allen, A. "Nature and Nurture: When It Comes to Twins, Sometimes It's Hard to Tell the Two Apart." *Washington Post,* Jan. 11, 1998.

Allport, G. *Pattern and Growth in Personality.* New York: Holt, Rinehart and Winston, 1961.

Andersen, S., Chen, S., and Miranda, R. "Significant Others and the Self." *Self and Identity,* 2002, *1,* 159–168.

Ashmore, R., and Jussim, L. (eds.). *Self and Identity* (Rutgers Series on Self and Identity, Vol. 1). Oxford, England: Oxford University Press, 1997.

Ashton, S. "Authenticity in Adult Learning." *International Journal of Lifelong Education,* 2010, *29*(1), 3–19.

Balaban, E. "Cognitive Developmental Biology: History, Process and Fortune's Wheel." *Cognition,* 2006, *101,* 298–332.

Bandura, A. *Principles of Behavior Modification*. New York: Holt, Rinehart and Winston, 1969.

Barnett, R. (ed.). *Reshaping the University: New Relationships Between Research, Scholarship and Teaching*. New York: SRHE and Open University Press, 2005.

Barnett, R. "Graduate Attributes in an Age of Uncertainty." In P. Hager and S. Holland (eds.), *Graduate Attributes, Learning and Employability*. Dordrecht, The Netherlands: Springer, 2006, 49–65.

Baumeister, R. F., and Alquist, J. L. "Is There a Downside to Good Self-Control?" *Self and Identity*, 2009, 8, 115–130.

Baumgartner, L. "White Whispers: Talking About Race in Adult Education." In V. Sheared et al. (eds.), *The Handbook of Race and Adult Education: A Resource for Dialogue on Racism*. San Francisco: Jossey-Bass, 2010, 105–118.

Baxter Magolda, M. "Developing Self-Authorship in Young Adult Life." *Journal of College Student Development*, 1998, 39, 143–156.

Baxter Magolda, M. *Making Their Own Way. Narratives for Transforming Higher Education to Promote Self-Development*. Sterling, VA: Stylus, 2001.

Bell, P. *Confronting Theory: The Psychology of Cultural Studies*. Chicago: University of Chicago Press, 2010.

Bellow, S. *Ravelstein*. London: Penguin Books, 2000.

Benn, S. I. "Freedom, Autonomy and the Concept of a Person." *Proceedings of the Aristotelian Society* (New Series), 1976, 76, 109–130.

Berger, P. L. *Invitation to Sociology*. New York: Doubleday, 1963.

Berger, P., and Luckmann, T. *The Social Construction of Reality*. London: Penguin Books, 1967.

Billett, S. "Situated Learning—a Workplace Experience." *Australian Journal of Adult and Community Education*, 1992, 34(2), 112–131.

Billett, S. "Situated Learning: Bridging Sociocultural and Cognitive Theorising." *Learning and Instruction*, 1996, 6, 263–280.

Billett, S. "Individualising the Social—Socialising the Individual: Interdependence Between Social and Individual Agency in Vocational Learning." Keynote address, 11th Annual International Conference on Post-Compulsory Education and Training, Enriching Learning Cultures, Gold Coast, Australia, Dec. 1–3, 2003.

Bingham, C. "On Paulo Freire's Debt to Psychoanalysis: Authority on the Side of Freedom." *Studies in Philosophy and Education*, 2002, 21, 447–464.

Blackman, L., Cromby, J., Hook, D., Papadopoulos, D., and Walkerdine, V. "Creating Subjectivities." *Subjectivity*, 2008, 22, 1–27.

Bouchard, T. J., and Loehlin, J. C. "Genes, Evolution, and Personality." *Behavior Genetics*, 2001, 31(3), 243–273.

Bouchard T. J., Lykken, D.T., McGue, M., Segal, N., and Tellegen, A. "Sources of Human Psychological Differences: The Minnesota Study of Twins Reared Apart." *Science*, 1990, 250, 223–228.

Boud, D., Cohen, R., and Walker, D. (eds.). *Using Experience for Learning*. Buckingham, England: The Society for Research into Higher Education and Open University, 1993.

Brookfield, S. D. "Using Critical Incidents to Explore Learners' Assumptions." In J. Mezirow and Associates, *Fostering Critical Reflection in Adulthood: A Guide to Transformative and Emancipatory Learning*. San Francisco: Jossey-Bass, 1991, 177–193.

Brookfield, S. D. *Becoming a Critically Reflective Teacher*. Hoboken, NJ: Wiley, 1995.

Brookfield, S. D. *The Power of Critical Theory: Liberating Adult Learning and Teaching*. San Francisco: Jossey-Bass, 2005.

Brookfield, S. D. "Authenticity and Power." In P. A. Cranton (ed.), *Authenticity in Teaching*. New Directions for Adult and Continuing Education, no. 111. San Francisco: Jossey-Bass, 2006, 5–16.

Brookfield, S. D. "Radical Questioning on the Long Walk to Freedom: Nelson Mandela and the Practice of Critical Reflection." *Adult Education Quarterly*, 2008, 58(2), 95–109.

Brookfield, S. D. "Engaging Critical Reflection in Corporate America." In J. Mezirow, E. Taylor, and Associates (eds.), *Transformative Learning in Practice: Insights from Community, Workplace and Higher Education*. San Francisco: Jossey-Bass, 2009, 125–135.

Brookfield, S. D. *Teaching for Critical Thinking: Tools and Techniques to Help Students Questions Their Assumptions*. San Francisco: Jossey-Bass, 2011.

Brookfield, S., and Holst, J. *Radicalizing Learning: Adult Education for a Just World*. San Francisco: Jossey-Bass, 2011.

Chappell, C., Rhodes, C., Solomon, N., Tennant, M., and Yates, L. *Reconstructing the Lifelong Learner: Pedagogies of Individual, Organizational and Social Change*. London: Routledge, 2003.

Christopher, J., Richardson, F., and Slife, B. (eds.). "Thinking Through Positive Psychology" (entire issue). *Theory and Psychology*, 2008, 18(5), 555–723.

Clark, C., and Rossiter, M. "Narrative Learning in Adulthood: Third Update on Adult Learning Theory." In S. B. Merriam (ed.), *Special Issue: Third Update on Adult Learning Theory*. New Directions for Adult and Continuing Education, no. 119. San Francisco: Jossey-Bass, 2008, 61–70.

Clendinnen, I. *Tiger's Eye*. Melbourne: Text, 2000.

Cloninger, C. R., Adolfsson, R., and Svrakic, N. M. "Mapping Genes for Human Personality." *Nature Genetics*, 1996, 12, 3–4.

Closson, R. "An Exploration of Critical Race Theory." In V. Sheared et al. (eds.), *The Handbook of Race and Adult Education: A Resource for Dialogue on Racism*. San Francisco: Jossey-Bass, 2010, 173–186.

Collins, M. *Adult Education as Vocation: A Critical Role for the Adult Educator*. London: Routledge, 1991.

Cooley, C. H. *Human Nature and the Social Order*. New York: Scribner, 1922.

Covey, S. *The 7 Habits of Highly Effective People*. Melbourne: Information Australia, 1989.

Cranton, P. "Individual Differences in Transformative Learning." In J. Mezirow and Associates (eds.), *Learning as Transformation: Critical Perspectives on Theory in Progress*. San Francisco: Jossey-Bass, 2000, 181–204.

Cranton, P. *Understanding and Promoting Transformative Learning* (2nd ed.). San Francisco: Jossey-Bass, 2006.

Crittenden, B. "Autonomy as an Aim of Education." In K. O. Strike and K. Egan (eds.), *Ethics and Educational Policy*. London: Routledge and Kegan Paul, 1978.

Cushman, P. "Why the Self Is Empty: Toward a Historically Situated Psychology." *American Psychologist*, 1990, 45(5), 599–611.

Daniels, H. *Vygotsky and Pedagogy*. London: Routledge-Falmer, 2001.

Danziger, K. "The Historical Formation of Selves." In R. Ashmore and L. Jussim (eds.), *Self and Identity* (Rutgers Series on Self and Identity, Vol. 1). Oxford, England: Oxford University Press, 1997, 137–159.

DeGloma, T. "Awakenings: Autobiography, Collective Memory, and the Social Geometry of Personal Discovery." Paper presented at the American Sociological Association Annual Meeting, Boston, 2008. www.allacademic.com/meta/p241345_index.html.

Dewey, J. *Experience and Education*. New York: Collier, 1963.

Dirkx, J. "Nurturing Soul in Adult Learning." In P. Cranton (ed.), *Transformational Learning in Action: Insights from Practice*. New Directions for Adult and Continuing Education, no. 74. San Francisco: Jossey-Bass, 1997, 79–88.

du Gay, P., Evans, J., and Redman, P. (eds.). *Identity: A Reader*. London: Sage, 2000.

Elman, J., Karmiloff-Smith, A., Bates, E., Johnson, M., Parisi, D., and Plunkett, K. *Rethinking Innateness: A Connectionist Perspective on Development*. Cambridge, MA: MIT Press, 1996.

Erikson, E. H. "Identity and the Life Cycle" (entire issue). *Psychological Issues*, 1959, *1*(1), 1–171.

Erikson, E. H. *Childhood and Society*. New York: Norton, 1963.

Erikson, E. H. *The Life Cycle Completed*. New York: Norton, 1982.

Eysenck, H. J. *The Structure of Human Personality*. London: Methuen, 1960.

Felman, S. "Psychoanalysis and Education: Teaching Terminable and Interminable." *The Pedagogical Imperative: Teaching as a Literary Genre* (Yale French Studies, no. 63). New Haven: Yale University Press, 1982, 21–44.

Fishbach, A., and Converse, B. "Identifying and Battling Temptation." In K. D. Vohs and R. F. Baumeister (eds.), *Handbook of Self-Regulation: Research, Theory, and Applications* (2nd ed.). New York: Guilford Press, 2010, 244–259.

Flavell, J. *The Developmental Psychology of Jean Piaget*. New York: Van Nostrand, 1963.

Foucault, M. *The History of Sexuality*. Vol. 3: *Care of the Self*. London: Penguin Books, 1988a.

Foucault, M. "Technologies of the Self." In L. Martin, H. Gutman, and P. Hutton (eds.), *Technologies of the Self: A Seminar with Michel Foucault*. Amherst: University of Massachusetts Press, 1988b, 16–49.

Foucault, M. "About the Beginnings of the Hermeneutics of the Self." *Political Theory*, 1993, *21*, 198–227.

Freire, P. *Pedagogy of the Oppressed*. London: Penguin Books, 1972.

Freire, P. *Education: The Practice of Freedom*. London: Writers and Readers, 1974.

Freud, A. *The Ego and the Mechanisms of Defense*, Trans. C. Baines. New York: International Universities Press, 1946.

Freud, A. *Psychoanalysis for Teachers and Parents*, Trans. B. Low. Boston: Beacon Press, 1960.

Freud, S. "Fragment of an Analysis of a Case of Hysteria." In J. Strachey (ed.), *The Standard Edition of the Complete Psychological Works of Sigmund Freud*, Vol. 7. London: Hogarth Press, 1953, 7–122.

Freud, S. "A Difficulty in the Path of Psychoanalysis." In J. Strachey (ed.), *The Standard Edition of the Complete Psychological Works of Sigmund Freud*, Vol. 17. London: Hogarth Press, 1954, 135–144.

Freud, S. "Some Reflections on Schoolboy Psychology." In J. Strachey (ed.), *The Standard Edition of the Complete Psychological Works of Sigmund Freud*, Vol. 13. London: Hogarth Press, 1955, 241–244.

Freud, S. "A Note on the Unconscious in Psychoanalysis." In J. Strachey (ed.), *The Standard Edition of the Complete Psychological Works of Sigmund Freud*, Vol. 12. London: Hogarth Press, 1958, 260–266.

Freud, S. *Civilization and Its Discontents*. London: Hogarth Press, 1963.

Freud, S. "New Introductory Lectures on Psychoanalysis. Lecture 34. Explanations, Applications and Orientations." In J. Strachey (ed.), *The Standard Edition of the Complete Psychological Works of Sigmund Freud*, Vol. 22. London: Hogarth Press, 1964, 136–157.

Freud, S. *Introductory Lectures on Psychoanalysis*. London: Penguin Books, 1973.

Fromm, E. *The Crisis of Psychoanalysis*. London: Penguin Books, 1973.

Gee, J. P. "Identity as an Analytic Lens for Research in Education." *Review of Research in Education*, 2000, *25*, 99–125.

Gergen, K. J., and Gergen, M. M. "Narrative and the Self as Relationship." In L. Berkowitz (ed.) *Advances in Experimental Social Psychology*, Vol. 21. New York: Academic Press, 1988, 17–56.

Gergen, K. J., and Kaye, J. "Beyond Narrative in the Negotiation of Therapeutic Meaning." In K. J. Gergen (ed.), *Refiguring Self and Psychology*. Aldershot, England: Dartmouth, 1993, 241–260.

Gibbs, B. "Autonomy and Authority in Education." *Journal of Philosophy of Education*, 1979, *13*, 119–132.

Gide, A. *The Immoralist*, Trans. D. Bussy. London: Penguin Books, 1902/1960.

Gilligan, C. *In a Different Voice*. Cambridge, MA: Harvard University Press, 1986.

Gleason, P. "Identifying Identity: A Semantic History." *Journal of American History*, 1983, 69(4), 910–931.

Goffman, E. *The Presentation of Self in Everyday Life*. London: Penguin Books, 1971.

Gross, J. J. (ed.). *Handbook of Emotion Regulation*. New York: Guilford Press, 2007.

Hall, S. "Introduction: Who Needs Identity?" In S. Hall and P. du Gay (eds.), *Questions of Cultural Identity*. London: Sage, 1997, 1–17.

Hateley, B., and Schmidt, W. H. *Pigeonholed in the Land of Penguins: A Tale of Seeing Beyond Stereotypes*. New York: AMACOM, 2000.

Heatherton, T. F., and Nichols, P. A. "Personal Accounts of Successful Versus Failed Attempts at Life Change." *Personality and Social Psychology Bulletin*, 1994, 20, 664–675.

"Here's Looking at You! The Know Yourself Seminar." LeaderWorks, n.d. www.leaderworks.com/knowyourself/quotes.html.

Hunt, C., and West, L. "Salvaging the Self in Adult Learning." *Studies in the Education of Adults*, 2009, 41(1), 68–82.

Hytten, K., and Warren, J. "Engaging Whiteness: How Racial Power Gets Reified in Education." *Qualitative Studies in Education*, 2003, 16(1), 65–89.

Illeris, K. *The Three Dimensions of Learning*. Leicester, England: NIACE, 2002.

Illeris, K. "A Comprehensive Understanding of Human Learning" In P. Jarvis and S. Parker (eds.), *Human Learning: A Holistic Approach*. London: Routledge, 2005, 87–100.

"I Traced My Dad . . . and Discovered He Is Charles Manson." *Sun*, Nov. 23, 2009. www.thesun.co.uk/sol/homepage/features/2740414/I-traced-my-dad-and-discovered-he-is-Charles-Manson.html.

Jahoda, M. *Current Concepts of Positive Mental Health*. New York: Basic Books, 1958.

James, W. *The Principles of Psychology*. New York: Henry Holt, 1890.

Jarvis, P. *Paradoxes of Learning: On Becoming an Individual in Society*. San Francisco: Jossey-Bass, 1992.

Jarvis, P. "Towards a Philosophy of Human Learning." In P. Jarvis and S. Parker (eds.), *Human Learning: An Holistic Approach*. London: Routledge, 2005, 1–15.

Jarvis. P. *Learning to Be a Person in Society*. London: Routledge, 2009.

Jung, C. G. *Memories, Dreams, Reflections*. London: Random House, 1967.

Kabat-Zinn, J. *Full Catastrophe Living: Using the Wisdom of Your Body and Mind to Face Stress, Pain and Illness*. New York: Dell, 1991.

Kafka, F. *The Metamorphosis*, Trans. K. Reppin. Prague: Vitalis, 1915/1996.

Kafka, F. "A Report to an Academy." In *The Metamorphosis, In the Penal Colony, and Other Stories*, Trans. W. Muir and E. Muir. New York: Schocken Books, 1948/1995, 173–183.

Kagitcibasi, C. "Autonomy and Relatedness in Cultural Context: Implications for Self and Family." *Journal of Cross-Cultural Psychology*, 2005, 36, 403–422.

Kellner, D. "Popular Culture and the Construction of Postmodern Identities." In S. Lash and J. Friedman (eds.), *Modernity and Identity*. Oxford, England: Blackwell, 1992, 141–177.

Klein, M. *Love, Gratitude and Other Works, 1921–1945*. London: Virago, 1998.

Knowles, M. *The Adult Learner: A Neglected Species*. Houston: Gulf, 1978.

Koestler, A. *The Ghost in the Machine*. London: Hutchinson, 1967.

Kontturi, K., and Tiainen, M. "Feminism, Art, Deleuze, and Darwin: An Interview with Elizabeth Grosz." *Nordic Journal of Women's Studies*, 2007, *15*(4), 246–256.

Koole, S., van Dillen, L., and Sheppes, G. "The Self-Regulation of Emotion." In K. D. Vohs and R. F. Baumeister (eds.), *Handbook of Self-Regulation: Research, Theory, and Applications* (2nd ed.). New York: Guilford Press, 2010, 22–40.

Kreber, C. "Courage and Compassion in the Striving for Authenticity: States of Complacency, Compliance, and Contestation." *Adult Education Quarterly*, 2010, *60*(2), 177–198.

Kreber, C., Klampfleitner, M., McCune, V., and Bayne, S. "What Do You Mean by 'Authentic'? A Comparative Review of the Literature on Conceptions of Authenticity in Teaching." *Adult Education Quarterly*, 2007, *58*(1), 22–43.

Larner, G. "Integrating Family Therapy in Child and Adolescent Mental Health Practice: An Ethic of Hospitality." *Australian and New Zealand Journal of Family Therapy*, 2003, *24*, 211–221.

Larner, G. *Deconstructing Therapy as Ethical Relation*. Unpublished doctoral thesis, University of Technology, Sydney, 2010.

Lave, J., and Wenger, E. *Situated Learning: Legitimate Peripheral Participation*. Cambridge, England: Cambridge University Press, 1991.

Leary, M., and Forest, W. "Editorial: Do We Need Another Journal? A Converted Skeptic's Reply." *Self and Identity*, 2002, *1*, 1–2.

Leary, M., and Tangney, J. "The Self as an Organizing Construct in the Behavioral and Social Sciences." In M. Leary and J. Tangney (eds.), *Handbook of Self and Identity*. New York: Guilford Press, 2003, 3–14.

Le Cornu, A. "Meaning, Internalization, and Externalization: Toward a Fuller Understanding of the Process of Reflection and Its Role in the Construction of the Self." *Adult Education Quarterly*, 2009, *59*(4), 279–297.

Levinson, D. *The Seasons of a Man's Life*. New York: Knopf, 1978.

Levinson, D. *The Seasons of a Woman's Life*. New York: Ballantine Books, 1996.

"Liu Xiaobo's Final Testimony." *Sydney Morning Herald*, Oct. 9, 2010.

Locke, J. *An Essay Concerning Human Understanding*. New York: Dover, 1694/1959.

Loevinger, J. *Ego Development*. San Francisco: Jossey-Bass, 1976.

Mandela, N. *Long Walk to Freedom*. New York: Little, Brown, 1994.

Mandela, N. *Conversations with Myself*. Sydney: Macmillan, 2010.

Marcuse, H. *Eros and Civilisation*. London: Sphere Books, 1969.

Martin, R. "Truth, Power, Self: An Interview with Michel Foucault." In L. Martin, H. Gutman, and P. Hutton (eds.), *Technologies of the Self: A Seminar with Michel Foucault*. Amherst: University of Massachusetts Press, 1988, 9–15.

Martin, L., Gutman, H., and Hutton, P. (eds.). *Technologies of the Self: A Seminar with Michel Foucault*. Amherst: University of Massachusetts Press, 1988.

Marx, K. *The Economic and Philosophical Manuscripts*. Marx/Engels Internet Archive, 1932/1993. www.marxists.org/archive/marx/works/1844/epm/index.htm.

Maslow, A. H. *Motivation and Personality*. New York: Harper & Row, 1954.

Maslow, A. *Towards a Psychology of Being*. New York: Van Nostrand, 1968.

Matusov, E. "When Solo Activity Is Not Privileged: Participation and Internalisation Models of Development." *Human Development*, 1998, *41*, 326–349.

May, T. "The Concept of Autonomy." *American Philosophical Quarterly*, 1994, *31*(2), 133–144

McAdams, D. *Power, Intimacy and the Life Story: Personological Inquiries into the Life Story*. New York: Guilford Press, 1985.

McAdams, D. *The Stories We Live By: Personal Myths and the Making of the Self*. New York: Morrow, 1993.

McAdams, D. "Personality, Modernity, and the Storied Self: A Contemporary Framework for Studying Persons." *Psychological Inquiry*, 1996, 7, 295–321.

McCrae, R. R., and Costa, P. T. "Personality Trait Structure as a Human Universal." *American Psychologist*, 1997, 52(5), 509–516.

McLaren, P. *Critical Pedagogy and Predatory Culture: Oppositional Politics in a Postmodern Era*. London: Routledge, 1995.

McWhinney, W., and Markos, L. "Transformative Education: Across the Threshold." *Journal of Transformative Education*, 2003, 1(1), 16–37.

Mead, G. H. *On Social Psychology: Selected Papers*, Ed. A. Strauss. Chicago: University of Chicago Press, 1934/1972.

Merriam, S., and Kim, Y. "Non-Western Perspectives on Learning and Knowing." In S. B. Merriam (ed.), *Special Issue: Third Update on Adult Learning Theory*. New Directions for Adult and Continuing Education, no. 119. San Francisco: Jossey-Bass, 2008, 71–81.

Mezirow, J. "On Critical Reflection." *Adult Education Quarterly*, 1998, 48(3), 185–198.

Mezirow, J. "Learning to Think Like an Adult: Core Concepts of Transformative Theory." In J. Mezirow and Associates (eds.), *Learning as Transformation: Critical Perspectives on Theory in Progress*. San Francisco: Jossey-Bass, 2000, 3–34.

Mezirow, J. "Transformative Learning as Discourse." *Journal of Transformative Education*, 2003, 1(1), 58–63.

Mezirow, J. "Transformative Learning Theory." In J. Mezirow, E. Taylor, and Associates (eds.), *Transformative Learning in Practice: Insights from Community, Workplace, and Higher Education*. San Francisco: Jossey-Bass, 2009, 18–31.

Mezirow, J., and Associates (eds.). *Learning as Transformation: Critical Perspectives on a Theory in Progress.* San Francisco: Jossey-Bass, 2000.

Mezirow, J., Taylor, E., and Associates. (eds.). *Transformative Learning in Practice: Insights from Community, Workplace, and Higher Education.* San Francisco: Jossey-Bass, 2009.

Musgrove, F. *Margins of the Mind.* London: Methuen, 1977.

Neville, R. C. "A Confucian Construction of a Self-Deceivable Self." In R. T. Ames and W. Dissanayake (eds.), *Self and Deception: A Cross-Cultural Philosophical Enquiry.* Albany: State University of New York Press, 1996, 201–217.

Newman, J. H. *The Idea of a University.* Washington DC: Regnery Gateway, 1999.

Newman, M. "The Self in Self-Development: A Rationalist Meditates." *Adult Education Quarterly,* 2008, 58(4), 284–298.

Newman, M. "Calling Transformative Learning into Question: Some Mutinous Thoughts" (Published online before print). *Adult Education Quarterly,* Dec. 20, 2010. doi: 10.1177/0741713610392768.

Nichols, W. C., and Schwartz, R. C. *Family Therapy Concepts and Methods* (6th ed.). Boston: Pearson Education, 2004.

Nixon, J. "Excellence and the Good Society." In A. Skelton (ed.), *International Perspectives on Teaching Excellence in Higher Education.* New York: Routledge, 2007, 23–53.

Organisation for Economic Cooperation and Development (OECD). *Investing in Competencies for All.* Paris: OECD, 2001.

Organisation for Economic Cooperation and Development (OECD). *The Definition and Selection of Key Competencies: Executive Summary.* Paris: OECD, 2003a.

Organisation for Economic Cooperation and Development (OECD). *The Definition and Selection of Competencies: Theoretical and Conceptual Foundations (DeSeCo): Summary of the Final Report.* Paris: OECD, 2003b.

Palmer, P. J. *The Courage to Teach: Exploring the Inner Landscape of a Teacher's Life*. San Francisco: Jossey-Bass, 1998.

Parker, I. "Psychoanalytic Theory and Psychology: Conditions of Possibility for Clinical and Cultural Practice." *Theory and Psychology*, 2008, *18*(2), 147–165.

Paxton, D. "Transforming White Consciousness." In V. Sheared et al. (eds.), *The Handbook of Race and Adult Education: A Resource for Dialogue on Racism*. San Francisco: Jossey-Bass, 2010, 119–132.

Peterson, C., Park, N., and Seligman, M. (2005). "Assessment of Character Strengths." In G. P. Koocher, J. C. Norcross, and S. S. Hill III (eds.), *Psychologists' Desk Reference* (2nd ed.). New York: Oxford University Press, 2005, 93–98.

Pinker, S. *The Blank Slate: The Modern Denial of Human Nature*. New York: Penguin Group, 2002.

Plato. *Protagoras*, Trans. B. Jowett. n.d. http://classics.mit.edu/Plato/protagoras .html.

Plummer, K. *Documents of Life 2: An Invitation to a Critical Humanism*. London: Sage, 2001.

Pratt, D., and Nesbit, T. "Discourses and Cultures of Teaching." In A. Wilson and E. Hayes (eds.), *Handbook of Adult and Continuing Education*. San Francisco: Jossey-Bass, 2000, 117–131.

Ratner, C. "Three Approaches to Cultural Psychology: A Critique." *Cultural Dynamics*, 1999, *11*, 7–31.

Reich, W. *The Sexual Revolution*. London: Vision Press, 1972.

Ridley, M. *Nature via Nurture: Genes, Experience, and What Makes Us Human*. HarperCollins, 2003.

Rimke, H. M. "Governing Citizens Through Self-Help Literature." *Cultural Studies*, 2000, *14*(1), 61–78.

Robbins, A. *Awaken the Giant Within: How to Take Immediate Control of Your Mental, Emotional, Physical and Financial Destiny.* New York: Simon & Schuster, 1992.

Rogers, C. R. *Client-Centered Therapy: Its Current Practice, Implications, and Theory.* Boston: Houghton Mifflin, 1951.

Rogers, C. R. *On Becoming a Person: A Therapist's View of Psychotherapy.* London: Constable, 1967.

Rogers, C. R. *Freedom to Learn for the 80s.* Columbus, OH: Merrill, 1983.

Rose, N. *Inventing Our Selves.* Cambridge, England: Cambridge University Press, 1998.

Rychen, D., and Salganik, L. (eds.). *Defining and Selecting Key Competencies.* Seattle: Hogrefe and Huber, 2001.

Salzberger-Wittenberg, I., Henry, G., and Osborne, E. *The Emotional Experience of Learning and Teaching.* London: Routledge and Kegan Paul, 1983.

Scott, S. "The Grieving Soul in the Transformative Process." In P. Cranton (ed.), *Transformational Learning in Action: Insights from Practice.* New Directions for Adult and Continuing Education, no. 74. San Francisco: Jossey-Bass, 1997, 41–50.

Seligman, M.E.P., and Csikszentmihalyi, M. (eds.). "Positive Psychology" (entire issue). *American Psychologist*, 2000a, 55(1), 1–183.

Seligman, M.E.P., and Csikszentmihalyi, M. "Positive Psychology: An Introduction." *American Psychologist*, 2000b, 55(1), 5–14.

Seligman, M.E.P., Steen, T. A., Park, N., and Peterson, C. "Positive Psychology Progress: Empirical Validation of Interventions." *American Psychologist*, 2005, 60(5), 410–421.

Shirts, G. "Bafa Bafa." Simulation Training Systems, 2009. www.simulation trainingsystems.com/business/bafa.html.

Shoda, Y., Mischel, W., and Peake, P. K. "Predicting Adolescent Cognitive and Self Regulatory Competencies from Preschool Delay of Gratification: Identifying Diagnostic Conditions." *Developmental Psychology*, 1990, *26*, 978–986.

Skinner, B. F. *Beyond Freedom and Dignity*. London: Penguin Books, 1973.

Slife, B. D., and Richardson, F. C. "Problematic Ontological Underpinnings of Positive Psychology: A Strong Relational Alternative." *Theory and Psychology*, 2008, *18*(5), 699–723.

Strachey, J. (ed.). *The Standard Edition of the Complete Psychological Works of Sigmund Freud*, Vols. 1–24. London: Hogarth Press, 1953–1974.

Sundararajan, L. "Toward a Reflexive Positive Psychology: Insights from the Chinese Buddhist Notion of Emptiness." *Theory and Psychology*, 2008, *18*(5), 655–674.

Tang, Y., and Posner, M. I. "Attention Training and Attention State Training." *Trends in Cognitive Science*, 2009, *13*, 222–227.

Tangney, J. P., Baumeister, R. F., and Boone, A. L. "High Self-Control Predicts Good Adjustment, Less Pathology, Better Grades, and Interpersonal Success." *Journal of Personality*, 2004, *72*, 271–324.

Taylor, K., Marienau, C., and Fiddler, M. (eds.). *Developing Adult Learners*. San Francisco: Jossey-Bass, 2000.

Tellegen, A. "Structure of Mood and Personality and Their Relevance to Assessing Anxiety, with an Emphasis on Self-Report." In A. H. Tuma and J. D. Maser (eds.), *Anxiety and the Anxiety Disorders*. Hillsdale, NJ: Erlbaum, 1985, 681–706.

Tennant, M. "Adult Education as a Technology of the Self." *International Journal of Lifelong Education*, 1998, *13*(4), 364–376.

Tennant, M. "Transforming Selves." *Journal of Transformative Education*, 2005, *3*(2), 102–115

Thompson, J. *Learning Liberation: Women's Response to Men's Education*. London: Croom Helm, 1983.

Tisdell, E. "Poststructuralist Feminist Pedagogies: The Possibilities and Limitations of Feminist Emancipatory Adult Learning Theory and Practice." *Adult Education Quarterly*, 1998, 48(3), 139–156.

Tisdell, E. "Spirituality and Adult Learning." In S. B. Merriam (ed.), *Special Issue: Third Update on Adult Learning Theory*. New Directions for Adult and Continuing Education, no. 119. San Francisco: Jossey-Bass, 2008, 27–36.

Tisdell, E. J., and Tolliver, D. E. "Transformative Approaches to Culturally Responsive Teaching: Engaging Cultural Imagination." In J. Mezirow, E. Taylor, and Associates (eds.), *Transformative Learning in Practice: Insights from Community, Workplace, and Higher Education*. San Francisco: Jossey-Bass, 2009, 88–99.

Usher, R., Bryant, I., and Johnson, R. *Adult Education and the Postmodern Challenge*. London: Routledge, 1997.

Usher, R., and Edwards, R. "Confessing All? A 'Postmodern' Guide to the Guidance and Counselling of Adult Learners." *Studies in the Education of Adults*, 1995, 27(1), 9–23.

Vaillant, G. *Adaptation to Life*. Boston: Little, Brown, 1977.

Valsiner, J. *Culture and the Development of Children's Action: A Theory of Human Development* (2nd ed.). Hoboken, NJ: Wiley, 1997.

Vanheule, S., and Verhaeghe, P. "Identity Through a Psychoanalytic Looking Glass." *Theory and Psychology*, 2009, 19(3), 391–411.

van Woerkom, M. "Critical Reflection as a Rationalistic Ideal." *Adult Education Quarterly*, 2010, 60(4), 339–356.

Vygotsky, L. S. *Mind in Society: The Development of Higher Psychological Processes*. Cambridge, MA: Harvard University Press, 1978.

Walker, M. "Pedagogies of Beginning." In M. Walker and J. Nixon (eds.), *Reclaiming Universities from a Runaway World*. Maidenhead, England: Society for Research into Higher Education and Open University Press, 2004, 131–146.

West, L., Alheit, P., Andersen, A., and Merrill, B. (eds.). *Using Biographical and Life History Approaches in the Study of Adult and Lifelong Learning: European Perspectives*. Frankfurt: Peter Lang, 2007.

White, M. *Selected Papers*. Adelaide, South Australia: Dulwich Centre, 1989.

White, M. "Deconstruction and Therapy." *Dulwich Centre Newsletter*, 1991, no. 3, 21–40.

Wiessner, C. A., Meyer, S. R., and Fuller, D. (eds.). *Challenges of Practice: Transformative Learning in Action*. Proceedings of the 3rd International Conference on Transformative Learning, Teachers College, Columbia University, 2000.

Winkler, R. "Heidegger and the Question of Man's Poverty in World." *International Journal of Philosophical Studies*, 2007, 15(4), 521–539.

Wulfert, E., Block, J. A., Santa Ana, E., Rodriguez, M. L., and Colsman, M. "Delay of Gratification: Impulsive Choices and Problem Behaviors in Early and Late Adolescence." *Journal of Personality*, 2002, 70(4), 533–552.

Yates, S., and Hiles, D. "Towards a 'Critical Ontology of Ourselves'? Foucault, Subjectivity and Discourse Analysis." *Theory and Psychology*, 2010, 20(1), 52–75.

Yourcenar, M. *Memoirs of Hadrian*. London: Penguin Books, 1959.

Zuckerman, M., and Cloninger, C. R. "Relationship Between Cloninger's, Zuckerman's and Eysenck's Dimensions of Personality." *Personality and Individual Differences*, 1996, 21, 283–285.

Index

Page references followed by *fig* indicate an illustrated figure; followed by *t* indicate a table.